Preaching

Preaching—pure and simple

Stuart Olyott

BRYNTIRION PRESS

© Stuart Olyott
First published 2005
Reprinted 2007

ISBN 13:978 1 85049 204 7

Biblical quotations are taken from the British usage text of
The Holy Bible, New King James Version
© Thomas Nelson Inc., 1982

Cover design: Evangelical Press

Published by Bryntirion Press
Bryntirion, Bridgend CF31 4DX, Wales, UK
Printed by Gomer Press, Llandysul, Ceredigion SA44 4QL

This book is dedicated to the memory of
Hugh David Morgan (1928–1992)
once described as
'the best-loved minister in Wales'

Contents

Introduction

JOHN is in his twenties and Jack is almost fifty, yet they have become good friends. They did not know each other until they met at a series of monthly preaching seminars in a nearby town. These monthly meetings not only gave to each man a new friendship, but they changed them for ever.

Before going to the seminars, John had never preached. It had been on his mind for a long time, but he had not known quite how to begin. After all, what exactly is preaching? What is the difference between a sermon and a 'talk'? Why is some preaching arresting and powerful, and some boring and flat? What are the essential elements of a good sermon? The seminars answered John's questions and put him on the right track. Today he preaches fairly regularly and a good deal of spiritual work has been done through his ministry.

Jack's story is quite different. Before going to the seminars he had been preaching for over twenty years, and yet he felt that he ought to be doing it better. He had read quite a few books on preaching. He had also asked a number of people for advice. Why, then, did his sermons not appear to feed anyone? Why did people switch off when he had been going only a few minutes? Most important of all, why did he know of so few people who had actually been changed by any of his sermons? To his intense relief, the seminars sorted him out. Many people now thank the Lord for Jack's powerful preaching of the Word.

The seminars were very modest affairs. Each one consisted of an introductory talk that said nothing new and owed a lot to the insights of others. This was followed by questions from the floor and half an hour of guided discussion. And yet the Johns and Jacks who attended those meetings constantly refer back to them and use their material to evaluate not only themselves, but also each other. They have asked that the substance of what they heard should be put into a brief book. So here it is.

STUART OLYOTT
Evangelical Movement of Wales
Bryntirion, Bridgend
March, 2005

PART ONE

What is preaching?

If someone spent a week reading through the Bible, and then a further week getting to grips with the main events of church history, what would they notice? They would notice that God's work in the world and preaching are intimately linked. Wherever God is at work, preaching flourishes. Wherever preaching is devalued or absent, the cause of God goes through a thin time. The kingdom of God and preaching are like conjoined twins who cannot be separated; they stand or fall together.

What does this mean for us? It means that if we have any serious desire to see God worshipped and loved more than he is, we will be passionately interested in the whole subject of preaching. This will be true whether we ourselves are preachers or not. If we preach, we will want to do it better. If we don't preach, we will want to do everything we can to help and encourage those who do.

So what *is* preaching? It is stunning to discover how very few people can give an accurate answer to this question. This is true even among those who have been preaching for years! The problem is that vast numbers of people have formed their ideas about preaching from what they have heard and read, rather than from a close study of the Bible.

Four New Testament words for preaching

The New Testament describes preaching in over sixty different ways, but it gives a special place to four great words.[1] In writing about them I shall use their verbal form, but I shall also have in mind other words which are in the same family. For example, when I use *kerusso*, 'to preach', I shall also have in mind *kerygma*, 'the message preached', and *keryx*, 'a herald'. So let us look at these four great words and see how they can help us to understand what preaching is. And perhaps some of us should prepare ourselves for a surprise!

(1) *kerusso*

There is no word for preaching which is more important than *kerusso*. It crops up wherever preaching is mentioned and is used more than sixty times. It means 'to declare as a herald does'. It refers to the message of a king. When a sovereign has a message for his subjects, he gives it to heralds. These heralds announce it to the people without altering or amending it in any way. They simply pass on the message that has been given to them. Their hearers know that they are receiving an official proclamation.

The New Testament uses this verb to emphasise that the preacher is not to announce his own words. He speaks for Someone Else. The stress is on the given-ness of the message. The preacher does not come on his own authority. He has been *sent*, and he speaks with the authority of the Sender. Words from the *kerusso* family are used to describe the preaching of Jonah (Matt. 12:41), of John the Baptist (Matt. 3:1), of our Lord Jesus Christ ('to proclaim', Luke 4:18b-19) and of his apostles ('a preacher', 1 Tim. 2:7; 2 Tim. 1:11).

---

[1] I first had my attention drawn to these four words by Dr Edmund P. Clowney's classic, *Preaching and Biblical Theology* (London, The Tyndale Press, 1962), pp. 54-9.

(2) *euangelizo*

This is the word from which we get our English verb 'to evangelise'. The Greek verb means 'to bring good news' or 'to announce good news'. When in Luke 2:10 the angel said, 'I bring you good tidings . . .', it was this verb he was using. But it is vital to notice straightaway that *kerusso* is not one thing while *euangelizo* is quite another. Many people have picked up the idea that these two verbs are talking about two separate activities. They have held on to this idea without ever studying what the Bible says on the subject. In this way they have developed very wrong views of preaching.

We need to look closely at Luke 4:18-19. In these verses our Lord is speaking in the synagogue of Nazareth, the Galilean town where he has been brought up. He begins his message by reading from the book of the prophet Isaiah. He chooses a passage which for hundreds of years has predicted his ministry. There is no doubt that his public reading was in Hebrew, but Luke's account of it is written in Greek. In verse 18a 'to preach the gospel' is a form of the verb *euangelizo*, while in verses 18b and 19 'to preach' is a form of the verb *kerusso*. Our Lord uses both verbs to describe his ministry. In doing one, he is doing the other. 'To herald' is 'to evangelise', and 'to evangelise' is 'to herald'!

'To evangelise' can even be used of something done to Christians! This can be seen, for example, in Romans 1:15. Having greeted his readers as believers in verse 7, and then given some other information in verses 8-14, Paul continues: 'So, as much as is in me, I am ready to preach the gospel to you who are in Rome also.' The expression 'to preach the gospel' is a translation of the verb *euangelizo*. Paul is coming to Rome to evangelise those who have already been converted! It is clearly time to think again about how we use our various words for preaching.

(3) *martureo*

This verb means 'to bear witness to facts'. But today when Christian people talk of 'witnessing', what do they usually mean? They frequently use the word to describe those moments when they tell others of their personal experience of the Lord. In the Bible *martureo* is not used in that way at all. Very often it is used of giving testimony in court. On other occasions it is used of calling on God (or even stones) to bear witness to something. It is all about *objectivity*, not subjectivity; it is telling people about facts and events, not about *my* feelings, or what happened to *me*.

Anyone who has spent time with the Septuagint (the ancient Greek translation of the Old Testament) knows that what I have just said is true. A study of the New Testament comes very quickly to the same conclusion. When the Samaritan woman uses *martureo* in John 4:39 ('testified') she is reporting the content of a conversation. When the apostle John uses *martureo* in 1 John 1:2 ('bear witness') he is reporting what he has seen and heard. When Paul uses *martureo* in Acts 26:5 ('to testify') it is because he is appealing for witnesses to appear in court.

But in studying this word there is one passage which is especially important. It is Luke 24:44-48. In these verses our resurrected Lord is telling his disciples what they are now to do. They are to go everywhere in the world heralding (*kerusso*) repentance and remission of sins (v.47, 'should be preached'), and witnessing (a word in the *martureo* family) to the great gospel facts as they do so (v.48).

14

Those who herald, bear witness; and those v.
ness, herald. And yet if we looked at Matthew 2.
would see that those who were given this G.
Commission were also told to *teach* (*didasko*).

Where is all this leading us? We have learned that *kerusso* is not something separate from *euangelizo*. We have also learned that *kerusso* is not something separate from *martureo*. And now we have just learned that neither *kerusso* nor *martureo* is something separate from *didasko*—our fourth great word, to which we will come in a moment.

Please note that I am not saying that these words are *interchangeable*. What I am showing is that when you do one of these things, you are doing the others as well—for preaching is *all* of these things! This is a point which cannot be stressed too strongly. We will underline it again later. In the meantime we must come to our fourth word.

(4) *didasko*

This word means 'to spell out in concrete terms what the message means as far as living is concerned'. It is a grave mistake to separate the *kerygma* (a word in the *kerusso* family) from the *didache* (a word in the *didasko* family). It is not just academic theologians who have tried to do this, for there are countless believers in our churches who make a clear distinction between a 'gospel message' and a 'teaching message'. We will say more about this in a few moments.

'Spelling out in concrete terms what the message means as far as living is concerned' is not to be something merely tagged on to our proclamation; it is to be part and parcel of the message that we herald. This is easily proved by reading through the Acts of the Apostles. In Acts 5:42 we read

.hat the apostles did not cease from 'teaching and preaching' (*didasko* and *euangelizo*) Jesus as the Christ. In Acts 15:35 we read that Paul and Barnabas spent time in Antioch 'teaching and preaching' (*didasko* and *euangelizo*) the word of the Lord. In Acts 28:31 we read that Paul used his home in Rome for 'preaching . . . and teaching' (*kerusso* and *didasko*). We need to be sensitive to the vocabulary of the inspired record; when someone is doing one of our verbs they are, at the same time, doing another of them!

There is more to be said than that. If we compare Acts 19:13 with 19:8 we see that when Paul was preaching (*kerusso*) in Ephesus, he was also 'speaking boldly', 'reasoning' and 'persuading'. In this way Luke shows that when someone heralds, they are doing very much more than our other three verbs express. To pursue this train of thought would take us into a study which is well beyond such a brief book as this. But before we leave the book of Acts we should perhaps take note of Acts 20:24-25. Here Paul explains to the Ephesian elders that bearing solemn witness to the gospel ('to testify to', a word in the *martureo* family) is something that has been happening while he has been 'preaching' (*kerusso*).

What this means for us

We are in danger of not seeing the wood for the trees. What is the real point that we are trying to make? It is this: when someone is preaching, wherever they are doing it and whoever they are speaking to, they are doing *all four* of the things that we have mentioned. In the New Testament we do not have one word for preaching to the lost and another word for preaching to the saved. We simply do not find messages known as 'teaching messages' while others are known as 'gospel messages'. Some readers may find this fact uncomfortable, but we cannot alter what the Bible says. Preaching, *all* preaching, is doing four things at once.

If we can see this, many passages of Scripture will strike us in a new way. A good example is 2 Timothy 4:1-5. In these verses Paul is writing his final words to a younger man who is already an important Christian leader. He solemnly instructs him to 'Preach the word!' At that point he uses the verb *kerusso*. But why is Timothy to do this? It is because the time is coming when people will not endure sound 'doctrine' (a word from the *didasko* family) and will heap up for themselves 'teachers' (another word from the *didasko* family). Paul is obviously telling Timothy that to preach (*kerusso*) is the way to teach (*didasko*) the church and to protect it from error.

But that is not all. Paul also tells Timothy to do the work of an 'evangelist' (a word from the *euangelizo* family). He means, of course, that as Timothy preaches (*kerusso*), and therefore teaches (*didasko*), he is to make sure that the true gospel (*euangelizo*) is kept to the forefront. And so we see in a single paragraph that three of our four words are used to describe Timothy's task. If he is a true preacher he will not be doing just one of these things, but all of them. Wherever true preaching is found, several things are happening at the same time.

If we do not take this on board we will never be true preachers. We must get rid of the idea that there are two species of preaching, one of which is suitable for the unconverted, and the other for the converted. From now on we must reject the thought that preaching to the lost and preaching to the saved are two different phenomena. We must not drive a wedge between preaching and preaching.

All preaching is the proclamation of salvation (in the fullest sense of that term) to men and women, boys and girls. It is true that the audiences may be vastly different. It is true that unconverted audiences and converted ones do not have the same needs. It is therefore true that the way the Word is applied may have to vary considerably. But it is *not* true that the preaching given to an unconverted audience is of a different breed to that given to a converted audience. The idea that there are two distinct types of preaching (and that some people are good at one type, while other people are good at the other type) is stopping people everywhere from understanding what true preaching is.

Our question answered

So what is preaching? Preaching, *all* preaching, is four things:

1. It is heralding a message given by the King (*kerusso*): this tells us about the *source* of the message and the *authority* with which it comes.

2. It is announcing good news (*euangelizo*): this tells us about the *quality* of the message and the *spirit* in which it is given.

3. It is bearing witness to facts (*martureo*): this tells us about the *nature* of the message and the *basis* on which it is constructed.

4. It is spelling out the implications of the message (*didasko*): this tells us about the *target* of the message (the hearer's conscience) and the *measure* of its success (did it change anyone's life?).

Until we are clear about this, we shall never really preach at all. So, to make things as plain as possible, will you come with me to a local church? There are not many people there and, as far as anyone can tell, they are all true believers. When I stand up to preach to them, what will I do?

First of all, I will get my message for them entirely from the Bible. I will not make it up. I will find out what the King says in his Word, and I will give them *that*. This is *kerusso*.

I may have to speak to them bluntly about their sin. That will be bad news. But I will not leave them in gloom and despair. I will show them how the passage leads them to Christ, and I will tell them who he is and what he has done for sinners. This will affect the spirit in which everything is said. Before the service ends, they will all have heard the good news of the grace of God. This is *euangelizo*.

My message will tell them about the date and times of the Bible book I am dealing with, and will give them plenty of factual information, whether it be about events, geography, culture, or whatever. Best of all, they will hear once more the great facts of the incarnation, life, death, resurrection and ascension of the Lord Jesus Christ. I will not leave them groping in an abstract world. This is *martureo*.

And I will speak directly to their consciences. I will show them what the passage means, but I will not stop there; I will show them what it means to *them*. They will know in what ways this passage demands a change in their life. In Christ's name, I will insist on repentance. I will give them Bible-based practical instructions. I will remind them of how, at last, they will answer to God himself. This is *didasko*.

I will have *preached*, because I will have done all four things that the Word of God requires of me. And then I will walk home. But on the way home, as likely as not, I will see a crowd of teenagers standing on a corner. Seeing that you are with me, I will stop to talk to them. We both know that we will have to put up with a few minutes of bored rudeness. We also know that they will eventually agree to listen to what we have to say. So where shall we start?

We will not invent what we are going to say to them. Although we may not have our printed Bibles open in front of their eyes, everything we say will come from the Book. We will transmit as faithfully as possible what the King has to say to young people like these. This is *kerusso*.

We will of course concentrate on the great truths of the gospel. We will tell these young people about God, about his demands, about his Son, and about their need to repent and believe. We will talk to them about God's wrath. We will gladly tell them about his love, and about what he did at the cross. We will love these youngsters as we speak to them. They will all know that our message is one of good news. This is *euangelizo*.

We won't get sidetracked from our task. We will tell them the facts about God's existence, about their sin, about the coming of Christ and his atonement and resurrection, about the end of the world, and about what God promises to those who turn to him. This is *martureo*.

We will press home our message with all the energy that we can. We will explain that they will be eternally lost if they stay as they are. We will command them, urge them, invite them and plead with them to repent of their sin and to turn to Christ. We will tell them that there is nothing more important than that. We will insist that they must do it now. This is *didasko*.

And so both in the church and on the street we will have done the same four things—*kerusso*, *euangelizo*, *martureo*, *didasko*. We will have given only one sermon, but we will have preached *twice*! We will have been in two vastly different situations, playing once at home and once away. We will have spoken to people who are very different to each other, but whose deepest needs are the same. We will have made different applications. We may well have had different results. But we will *not* have done two different things. Despite the enormous differences in the situations, on both occasions we will have been *preaching*!

Some key features of New Testament preaching

It is clear, then, what preaching *is*. We now know enough about it to discover whether we are really doing it or not. We also now know about the spirit in which it should be done. But it would be wrong to close an introductory chapter like this without flagging up that the New Testament underlines three particular features of true preaching.

(1) Compulsion

The first is *compulsion*. There is something inside the preacher that propels him into this work. He has an inner constraint that is bigger than he is. There is a fire in his heart which refuses to go out. He can't help it. He *must* preach. He cries out, 'Woe is me if I do not preach the gospel!' (1 Cor. 9:16). When commanded to stop, he declares with the apostles, 'We cannot but speak the things which we have seen and heard' (Acts 4:20). He has a sense of destiny which has no trouble in understanding what his Lord meant when he said, 'Let us go into the next towns, that I may preach there also, because for this purpose I have come forth' (Mark 1:38).

Where there is no inner coercion, there is no true preaching. In the Bible, the man who heralds, proclaims, bears witness to facts and targets the conscience, is a man who is *driven*. In the depths of his soul his God has conquered him, and he lives every waking hour with the consciousness that he has been *sent*. The experience is so deep that he has no words to describe it. The best he can do is to talk about his 'call', although he has never heard a voice or seen a vision.

In all normal circumstances, the 'call' of the preacher is eventually recognised, in one way or another, by the church of Jesus Christ. This recognition is often referred to as 'the outward call'. It would be unusual for anyone to continue preaching without it. But sometimes the professing church is so undiscerning, so immature, so worldly and so sinful, that it is quite incapable of recognising a heaven-sent man. The man who is truly called will not be put off by this. The God-given fire will burn as brightly as ever. The inner energy will drive him on. He will preach, and preach, and preach again, because the compulsion inside him is invincible and it leaves him no option.

(2) Plainness

The second key feature is *plainness*. Of course it is! Heralds always speak in the language of the people in front of them. Good news which is wrapped up in difficult words and phrases is not good news. If facts are not presented clearly, they will sound like fiction. And how can anything be pressed on the conscience if it is not understood?

True preachers are plain preachers. They declare the word of the King, and so do not draw attention to themselves. They do not allow anything to dim or obscure the message of the cross. They are anxious that every hearer should register the facts and not be distracted by the way they are presented. They are determined that no one will be in any doubt about what is expected of them next.

The apostle Paul speaks for every true preacher of the Word when he describes his preaching as an open statement of the truth (2 Cor. 4:2). He has made up his mind 'to preach the gospel, not with wisdom of words, lest the cross of Christ should be made of no effect' (1 Cor. 1:17). His description of his ministry runs like this:

> And I, brethren, when I came to you, did not come with excellence of speech or of wisdom declaring to you the testimony of God. For I determined not to know anything among you except Jesus Christ and him crucified. I was with you in weakness, in fear, and in much trembling. And my speech and my preaching were not with persuasive words of human wisdom, but in demonstration of the Spirit and of power, that your faith should not be in the wisdom of men but in the power of God.
>
> (1 Cor. 2:1-5)

(3) Christ-centredness

The third key feature is Christ-centredness. It has to be. This is because preachers are heralds of the Scriptures, and all the Scriptures are about Christ. Explicitly or implicitly, directly or indirectly, every single part of the Bible points us to him. There is no passage in the whole Book which is an exception.

It was the Spirit of Christ that moved every Old Testament author to write what he wrote (1 Peter 1:10-12). It was the Lord Jesus Christ himself who opened the Old Testament to his disciples and explained to them that he was in it everywhere (Luke 24:25-27,44-48). The four Gospels and the Acts, all the epistles and the Revelation, also have him as their great subject. So what shall we say about a preacher who opens the Bible and does not preach

Christ from the passage in front of him? Such a preacher has not understood the Book; and if he has not understood the Book, he should not be preaching!

The Lord Jesus Christ is the sum and the centre of all that God has revealed in his Word. He is the focus of the Bible's storyline. He is in the heart of every writer, unveiling himself to their mind and so guiding their pen. He reveals himself through the Bible's pages to every person that he has personally commissioned to preach. Where he is not preached there has been no preaching at all.

Why this book is set out as it is

With all these things in mind, we are now in a position to understand why this book is set out as it is. We now know what preaching is. We have seen three of its key features. So how do we set about doing it? And how can we be sure of doing it well?

It is not difficult to answer these questions. Seeing that we are heralds of the King, and everything he has to say is in his Book, there can be nothing more important than getting its meaning right. And we have not got its meaning right if we have not seen Christ there. Preaching requires *exegetical accuracy*.

The Bible, however, is a complete book. Nothing can now be added to it. This being so, we can study its pages and work out what it teaches on a particular subject. In doing so we find that it teaches a whole system of doctrine. Any passage on which I preach reveals part of that system, so I must tell the people what that is. Preaching requires *doctrinal substance*.

But haven't we learned that plainness is a key feature of biblical preaching? Can a message be called plain if it is difficult to follow and impossible to remember? Preaching requires *clear structure*. And, for the same reason, it requires *vivid illustration*.

We must not forget that the King's word, the good news, built as it is on facts, must be addressed to the conscience (*didasko*). It insists that every hearer should put their life right. Preaching requires *pointed application*.

Come what may, the divine message must get across. Nothing must be allowed to get in the way. The way the preacher speaks and moves can either be a help or a hindrance. Preaching requires *helpful delivery*.

Because of the inward fire which refuses to die down, the preacher will certainly be emotionally engaged as he speaks. He will speak the King's word in the King's name, but he will not want to do so without experiencing the King's presence and blessing. There is a dimension in true preaching that we dare not overlook. Preaching requires *supernatural authority*.

These are the elements which make up true preaching. It is not enough to have most of them; we need them all. We also need a method of preparing sermons which, as far as possible, makes sure of this. And so our book closes with a section that outlines a suggested method of preparing to preach, which is followed by a tribute to a preacher who exemplified the principles outlined in this book.

PART TWO

What makes good preaching?

1
Exegetical Accuracy

Our task, then, is clear: we are to use our mouths to explain and proclaim the Word of God and to apply it to the consciences and lives of the people in front of us.

But where is the Word of God to be found? All that God has to say to men and women has been written down in the words and sentences that make up the Bible. Those words and sentences have an intended meaning. Nothing, then—nothing at all!—can be more important than getting that meaning right. Study which brings out the intended meaning of words and sentences is called exegesis. No preaching is true preaching unless everything that is said is built on a foundation of *exegetical accuracy*.

It is a sin to preach what we think the Scriptures mean rather their intended meaning. It is equally a sin to preach the thoughts that the Word triggers in our own minds, rather than what the Word actually declares. A herald is a traitor if he does not convey *exactly* what the King says. Who will dare to stand before a congregation and proclaim 'Thus says the Lord!' and then proceed to say in the Lord's name what he has *not* said? It needs to be stressed again and again: there is nothing in preaching—nothing at all!—that is more important than exegetical accuracy.

When is 'exegesis' *not* exegesis?
We must not think, however, that all preachers who spend long hours studying the Bible are good exegetes.

Prayer, time and effort must be married to proper principles of interpretation. Many sincere people misunderstand the Bible completely. They then stand up and lead their hearers into error. This will not do.[1]

(a) Superstition

Some people, for example, study the Bible *superstitiously*. Instead of focusing on the plain sense of the words and sentences on the page, they are constantly looking for hidden meanings. What is written on the face of Scripture does not move them particularly, but they are thrilled to bits if they can see something there that ordinary people cannot see! For them this is the 'spiritual' meaning of Scripture, and it is much more important than the plain meaning.

Among those who study the Bible like this are people who pay great attention to the numerical value of Hebrew letters. Most of the Old Testament was written in Hebrew. Each letter of the Hebrew alphabet serves not only as a letter, but also as a number. If you like, you can add up the numbers represented by the letters of a word, and you can then give that word a numerical value. You can do the same with sentences. You may then be able to find other letters or sentences with the same numerical value, and so on. With all these numbers in front of you, and with a little imagination, you can come to all sorts of conclusions! Think of what you might be able to say to people after a study of all the words and sentences with a numerical value of 666!

[1] Some of this section is based on a lecture by Dr Ernest F. Kevan that I heard when I was a theological student. Extracts from that lecture had been previously published as Kevan, Ernest F., 'The Principles of Interpretation', in Carl F. Henry (ed.), *Revelation and the Bible* (London, The Tyndale Press, 1959), pp. 283-98.

Other people do not go as far as this, but they are controlled by the same mindset. If they are not interested in Hebrew letters, they may well be fascinated by the meaning of Bible place-names, on which they base a great deal of their teaching. For them, it is the meaning which ordinary people cannot see that is the important one. 'After all,' they argue, 'doesn't 1 Corinthians 2:14 teach us that spiritual things are to be understood spiritually?'

The fact that they can use that verse as they do shows what defective exegetes they are! In that verse Paul is talking about unconverted people. He is teaching that they do not welcome spiritual things. They don't want anything to do with them. They think that spiritual things are foolish and irrelevant. This is because they do not have any spiritual senses. You have got to have a change of nature, you have got to receive a new heart, before you can appreciate spiritual things.

The Bible does not teach that its pages can only be understood by a spiritual elite, and it certainly does not claim that its true meaning is the one that most people can't find! True preachers of the Word reject all superstitious approaches to exegesis.

(b) Allegory

Some people study the Bible *allegorically*. Their way of thinking has some similarities to the one we have just described, but it is not identical. They are genuinely interested in the plain grammatical sense of God's Word, but believe that in addition to that there is something *more* to be discovered.

People have been studying the Bible in an allegorical way ever since the earliest centuries of the Christian church. To understand how they tick we should perhaps think of John Bunyan's great book *The Pilgrim's Progress*. In that book we meet a whole range of characters who have the most extraordinary adventures. These characters and adventures are important, because without them the book would have no existence. What really matters, however, is not the details of the story, but what Bunyan is getting at as he tells us that story. He has truths to teach. He has lessons for us to learn. These are the things that count, and not the characters and adventures which are used to get them across.

Those who study the Bible allegorically read it in a very similar way. The plain meaning of the words and sentences is important, but not nearly as important as the truths and lessons which lie behind it. The Bible is full of meanings, and the plain meaning is among the least valuable.

This approach leads to unlimited fantasy and to the wildest possible interpretations. The Old Testament in particular is made to mean just whatever the preacher wants it to mean. This method of 'exegesis' kills serious study. It rewards ingenuity. Preaching becomes just a display of the preacher's inventive powers, while the difficult plodding required by serious exegesis disappears from the scene.

I once heard a thrilling sermon on Genesis chapter 24. I sat on the edge of my seat for seventy-five minutes and was completely enthralled as the preacher told the story of how Abraham sent his trusted servant to Mesopotamia to find a wife for his son Isaac. The purpose of the sermon was to show us how God the Father brings home a bride for his Son. In the sermon Abraham equalled God the Father, Isaac equalled God the Son, the servant equalled the Holy Spirit, Rebekah equalled the church, and the camels equalled the divine promises which carry the Spirit-led church safely to heaven!

It is forty years since I heard that sermon and I can remember it almost word for word. It was preached by a man of God to whom I owe more than I can ever express. He has been in heaven for years and I do not intend to tarnish his memory in any way at all. His sermon would have been all right if he had simply used Genesis 24 as an illustration of the doctrine he was teaching. But he did not. He definitely gave the impression that Genesis 24 is *intended* to teach how God the Father brings home a bride for his Son. But that is not its intended meaning at all. And so, sadly, I have to say that a sermon which left me spellbound was a bad sermon.

True preaching requires us to bring out the *intended meaning* of the passage we are dealing with. There is no place for allegorising, unless we are clearly telling people that our only reason for doing it is to illustrate a point—and it must be a point that we have already made by the route of proper exegesis. It is no use appealing to passages like Galatians 4:21-31 to argue that allegory is sometimes permitted. Some people also mention 1 Corinthians 10:1-3 and Hebrews 7:1-3 in support of this view. If we look closely at these passages we will see that they are not allegories at all, although that is what they appear to be on first sight. They are examples of how the Old Testament can be used by way of illustration. It is also interesting to note that none of these passages is used to prove any sort of doctrine.

It is time to turn our back on allegorising. There is a simple question that will tell us whether our use of a passage is allegorical or illustrational: in studying my passage, has the *intended meaning* of its words and sentences come to the front of the stage, or has it retreated into the background? If the intended meaning is not right at the forefront, allegory is lurking around dangerously somewhere—and it must be killed off right away!

(c) Dogma

There is another group of people who study the Bible *dog-matically*. There is nothing wrong with dogma, as long as we understand what it is. It is not a word that I like very much because it is old-fashioned and, as far as most people are concerned, it sends out unwelcome signals. 'Dogma' is an outdated word for doctrine. 'Dogmatic theology' is another way of describing 'systematic theology'. But what on earth is that? It is the statement of that system of doctrine taught in the Bible, without using any data apart from that which the Bible itself provides.

The most powerful preachers have always been those who are strong in dogmatic theology. They embrace a system which rules them completely. It decides their beliefs and governs their behaviour. It is echoed in their prayers and comes across clearly in their preaching. They are men of conviction, and this is precisely why they are in danger.

As they study any part of the Bible, it is easy for these men to interpret it in the light of their system, rather than to remember that it is the Bible itself which is the source of that system. The fact is that some passages of the Scriptures are very difficult to understand. We are tempted to make them 'fit' our system, rather than to take the time and trouble necessary to get down to some rigorous exegesis. Many preachers who are strong in dogmatic theology fall into this trap. We can even say that they fall into it regularly. They make certain texts and passages appear to say things which, in fact, they do *not* say!

We can take Hebrews 6:4-8 as an example. Countless preachers and commentaries have interpreted these verses in the light of their system and have therefore failed to understand them properly. Those who have a system which teaches that true Christians can be lost use these verses to prove their point. Those whose system teaches that a true Christian can never be lost say that the warning given in these verses is only hypothetical—the author is painting a frightening picture, but he is not talking about reality.

In both cases a dogmatic approach to Scripture leads its followers into error. If either of these views were preached, the preacher would be guilty of exegetical *in*accuracy. The passage is not commenting on whether Christians can be lost or not. That is not its purpose. But the situation it speaks about is certainly not hypothetical, as verse 9 makes so clear. The passage is one of several in the Epistle to the Hebrews which are intended to show that it is possible to have a *true* experience of the Holy Spirit without necessarily having a *saving* experience. The proof that you have had a saving experience of the Holy Spirit is not that you have felt something, but that you continue in the faith and bear fruit. If that doesn't happen, you will be lost—so you had better get your act together and take concrete steps to ensure your spiritual progress.

Only a commitment to thorough exegesis can preach the intended meaning of the passage. And what is true of Hebrews 6:4-8 is true of every other part of the Bible. Dogmatic theology is good, but we must learn to keep it in its place. If we don't, it will ruin our preaching.

(d) Human reason
I would like to conclude this section by mentioning that there are people who study the Bible *rationalistically*. The

big thing for them is human reason and they reject everything that offends it, which means, of course, that they do
not believe in miracles or any form of supernatural phenomena. These people are sure that there is truth in the Bible,
but they cannot bring themselves to believe that every part
of it is true. How could it be? Wasn't the Bible written by
imperfect men?

Such an approach has a massive effect on the way the
Bible is interpreted. Moses and the Israelites can't have
crossed the Red Sea in the way that Exodus describes,
because who can believe that the waters stood as a wall on
either side of them? Can we really believe that Isaiah predicted the rise of Cyrus *by name* long, long before he was
born? The feeding of the five thousand must be explained
in some other way, as must the physical resurrection of our
Lord Jesus Christ.

One of the ways that a trust in human reason has dis-
played itself in recent years has been by the attempt to
'demythologise' the Bible, and the Gospels in particular.
The idea is that when the four authors wrote their Gospels
in the first century, they could only think in the way that
first-century people did. To understand what they were getting at, we must strip off their first-century way of looking
at things and look at the underlying truths in a twenty-first-
century manner. For example, we don't have to believe that
Jesus rose physically from the dead; it is enough to believe
that through the Jesus experience men and women may
have real life. The story of his ascension is not to be taken
literally; what is happening is that the Gospel writers are
pointing us to the 'otherness' of Jesus.

What shall say about all this? We reject this approach,
and we reject it totally. The Bible, although penned by
imperfect men, is the Word of God. He has breathed it out,

and guaranteed that its human authors wrote it down accurately, without in any way crushing their personalities or their distinctive styles. The Bible is supernatural in its origin. If we take everything supernatural out of it, it has no message. We must understand the Old Testament as our Lord understood it, and we must believe and submit to the New Testament as the Scriptures he commissioned his apostles to write.

If we throw out everything which baffles human reason, we will be guilty of exegetical distortion. We will end up preaching nothing but our own ideas. Rejection of the supernatural reduces the Bible to nonsense, and the preacher can make it say just whatever he wants. Principles of interpretation which are entirely man-centred will never succeed in understanding the Book of God. No true exegesis, and therefore no true preaching, will ever come out of the rationalistic camp.

What principles should govern the exegete?

What principles, then, should I adopt if I am to discover what the passage before me is actually saying? How *do* I find out its intended meaning, and therefore have something to preach?

Many books have been written on this subject and those which are longest are not necessarily the best. This little book on preaching cannot possibly summarise what any of them has to say. All it can do is underline a few points. It can draw your attention to what is basic. It can stop you falling into the abyss of exegetical disaster and can place your feet on ground which is safe and sure.

To avoid ruining both yourself and your hearers you must always ask and answer seven questions before you preach on any passage of God's Word. Take time! Don't study in order to get a sermon—no! no!—but study in order to understand the text. *This is the rule above all rules that preachers must respect*. The sermon that you eventually preach must be quite a small thing compared with the great work that you undertake in the secret place.

(1) What does God expect of me as I take on this work?

He expects me to remember that the Book I am studying is his holy Word. He expects me to gaze at it in wonder and to whisper in awe, 'God has spoken *here*! . . . God is speaking *here*!' He expects me to open it with worship, amazement, gratitude and reverence. The very depths of my soul are to be ravished by the thought that I am in the presence of a divine revelation. This is a holy moment. Tears would not be out of place. Nor would a cry of joy.

He expects me to believe everything that I read. He expects me to talk to him as I do that reading. He expects me to treasure everything in my heart, to find it sweeter than honey and more precious than gold. He expects me to renew my vows to put it all into practice.

He expects me to remember that he has given this Book to be a revelation. It therefore has a meaning. Yes, the passage I am reading has a meaning. The human author, however, was aware not only of the meaning that he intended (which I have got to discover), but also that his words carried a meaning much fuller then he himself could grasp. He was aware that he was writing to address a particular situation, but also that his words were for the whole worldwide church of Christ throughout all generations. How do I know this? Because 1 Peter 1:10-12 teaches it. The Lord expects me to remember that as well.

He expects me to come to his Word without any pre-conceived notions about what it *ought* to say, but to humbly and obediently discover what it actually *does* say. He expects me to remember that I am a creature whose understanding is very limited; not only so, but I am a sinner whose ability to understand has been severely spoiled. He expects me to admit that I will never understand his Book without his personal help. He expects me to ask him for it.

The Bible can be studied by a man at his desk. But that man cannot be a true exegete, and a true preacher, unless in his heart he is studying on his knees. Exegesis is hard work. It is a self-imposed academic discipline. But, before all that, it is an act of worship.

(2) What is the grammatical meaning of the words?

God's Holy Book is made up words. Some of those words are nouns, others are verbs, and there are also articles, adjectives, adverbs, numerals, pronouns, prepositions, conjunctions, interjections and a good deal beside. The nouns may be singular, dual or plural. The verbs can be in a variety of strengths, tenses, moods and voices. And all these words are arranged into sentences, and the way they are arranged gives that sentence a *meaning*!

We should not be frightened by this. You have a book in your hand which you have been reading for quite a while now. It, too, is made up of words of various sorts, arranged into sentences, and all with a view to getting something from my mind into yours. If I had used different words, or if I had arranged the same ones in another way, you would have picked up a different meaning. So grammar is important. It is impossible to write a book without it.

In the same way every sentence in the Bible has a meaning. If the words were different, or the grammar was changed, it would have a different meaning. So, whether we like it or not, we cannot have exegetical accuracy without giving careful attention to individual words and to the way that they are arranged into sentences. That is what exegesis is about.

Preachers must learn to love grammar! They must make the effort to understand how language functions. If they don't, it is impossible for them to do their work. It is true that the Bible is a divinely inspired book. But it is still a book. And it must be read like a book. We must respect the basic grammatical sense of its words and phrases. This, of course, may be affected by the sort of literature in which those words and phrases are found—and this is a point that we shall explore in a moment. But we must face the fact: exegesis can only be done by people who take the Bible at its face value and who accept its words and sentences in their normal meaning.

It is my privilege at this stage of my life to travel quite widely and to meet a lot of preachers. I am sorry to tell you that countless numbers of them have been infected by a worldwide epidemic of grammatical carelessness. They don't know about grammar, don't care about it, and don't pay much attention to it as they study the biblical passages from which they are going to preach. Yet almost all the preachers I know believe that the divine inspiration of the Bible extends to each single word! There is something seriously wrong and it is high time to put it right.

(3) In what particular literary style are these words found?

Words do not exist on their own. Even a simple 'No!' is a response to something that has just been said. Every word has a context. Something has gone before it and something will follow it. We are not just talking about phrases and sentences, but also about the sort of literature in which those phrases and sentences are found. This is also something to which we must give careful attention as we seek to find out the intended meaning of any particular part of God's Word.

There are a lot of laws in the Bible, especially in the earlier part of the Old Testament. Laws are written in plain prose. So are historical records. But the style we use when speaking to each other is very different indeed. We liven up our conversation with all sorts of word-pictures—'She had a face like thunder', 'He pulled himself up by his bootlaces', 'They hit the deck', 'He's a beast'. We all know that these expressions are not to be taken literally (did he *really* pull on his laces and levitate?), but nor do we miss their meaning. So it is quite plain that legal prose and personal conversation are not to be interpreted in the same way, and this is also true as we read the Bible.

We simply cannot interpret every sort of literature in the same way. Besides the legal and historical prose we have mentioned, there is a lot of poetry in the Bible, some of it in books like Job, the Psalms or the Song of Solomon, some of it in the prophets, and some of it found as shorter or longer sections in other books. In addition we find Wisdom Literature, Gospels and epistles. There is also apocalyptic language—a way of making a point by using exaggerated language, numbers, pictures of monsters and extraordinary visions. If we were to read all these sorts of literature in the same way we would get very muddled indeed!

Whatever sort of literature we have in front of us, we must never forget to give attention to the plain grammatical sense of everything we read. But in doing so we must take time to call to mind that the *literal* meaning of a passage may not necessarily be its *intended* meaning, and it is that *intended* meaning we are looking for.

For example, in writing about a time of extraordinary joy Isaiah predicted: 'all the trees of the field shall clap their hands' (Isaiah 55:12). What did he mean? He was certainly not declaring that trees would develop amazing new qualities in some future century! In the same way, 'The righteous shall flourish like a palm tree' (Psalm 92:12) is not teaching that godly old people will sprout, while 'Beware of false prophets, who come to you in sheep's clothing' (Matt. 7:15) is not a warning about preachers who wear sweaters! We cannot understand these statements without grasping the grammatical sense of their words, but none of us is naïve enough to think that their literal meaning is their *intended* meaning—and it is that intended meaning which our exegesis sets out to discover, and which we then preach in public.

(4) What is the immediate and wider context?

Words are found in phrases and sentences, and sentences are usually found in paragraphs. These paragraphs, in turn, are part of something bigger, such as a chapter; and the chapters are part of a book. This, too, we must call to mind as we apply ourselves to our exegesis.

If we ignore the immediate and wider context, we can make the Bible say anything we want it to say. The material that makes up this book on preaching was originally given in spoken form. All of the addresses were recorded. Now let's imagine someone buying a cassette or CD and spending time editing it. Let's imagine that he keeps each sentence intact, but that he uses his electronic equipment to put those sentences in a different order. Having done that, he puts an advert in a Christian paper and starts selling cassettes and CDs of his own.

The voice on the recordings would be mine. Each sentence would be mine, exactly as I spoke it. But the spoken address would be completely different. It would either sound like a jumble of incoherent sentences, or it would have a meaning entirely different to the one I originally intended.

This is precisely what happens when we preach on any phrase or sentence of the Bible without being clear about its immediate and wider context. How many times have you heard 'You must be born again' (John 3:7) preached as if it were a *command*? This is a complete distortion of its meaning. To preach those words as a command is to mislead every adult and child who is listening. The new birth is not commanded anywhere in the Bible. Repentance is commanded. Faith in our Lord Jesus Christ is commanded. But the new birth is not (and cannot be) commanded, because it is entirely a work of God. When our Lord said to Nicodemus, 'You must be born again', he was making a blunt statement of fact. That is the point to be stressed to any congregation hearing those words today. To preach any other meaning is not only a lack of exegetical accuracy; it is sin.

On several occasions I have heard sermons mention 1 Corinthians 2:9, a verse where Paul refers to Isaiah 64:4. The main part of the verse reads like this: 'Eye has not seen, nor ear heard, nor have entered into the heart of man the things which God has prepared for those who love him.' Every preacher I have heard has used these words to talk about heaven. They have done this because they have

43

taken these words out of their context. 1 Corinthians chapter 2 is not about heaven; it is about the fact that the Lord's people can see and appreciate things that are hidden from unconverted people. What an extraordinary privilege we have! What wonderful things we see! The unconverted heart can't even begin to imagine them, and yet they are the things that thrill us through and through. *This* is what the verse is about, and it is both ungodly and wrong to give it a meaning that the Divine Author does not intend it to have.

The only way we can avoid exegetical error is by doing a lot more work. Before we preach on any *part* of a biblical book we should have a good acquaintance with the whole of it. Not only so, but we should have a competent understanding of who wrote it, to whom, why and when. The issue of *when* is particularly important, which is why we need to ask our next question.

(5) What is the historical setting?

The Bible mentions literally thousands of events and they did not all happen at the same time. It mentions thousands of people and they did not all live at the same time. It teaches thousands of truths but they were not all revealed at the same time. There is a great storyline that every preacher must know both in outline and in detail. He needs to be clear about what happened when. And he needs to be able to make a mark on any point of the storyline and to be able to say what had been revealed up to that point, and what was going to be revealed later.

If he can't do this easily he is heading for exegetical disaster, and the effect of his ministry on others will be catastrophic. God is filled with grace, but his grace has not always been dispensed to men and women in the same way. There are striking similarities and yet vast differences between an outline drawing, a full sketch, a painted picture and a colour film, but that is how God unveiled his great plan of redemption through the centuries. The beginning of Old Testament history is not the same as the middle or the end. The Old Testament is not the New. Shadow is not substance. The situation in the Gospels is not the same as what preceded or followed. Believers before Pentecost are not the same as those afterwards. The church at the beginning of Acts is not as mature or international as it is at the end. The church on earth does not yet enjoy what it will enjoy after Christ's second coming.

In Job 19:25-27 the suffering saint exclaims: 'I know that my Redeemer lives, and he shall stand at last on the earth; and after my skin is destroyed, this I know, that in my flesh I shall see God, whom I shall see for myself, and my eyes shall behold, and not another.' If we know where Job fits on the great storyline, we can begin to appreciate what an extraordinary statement this is. But if Job said this after Paul wrote 1 Corinthians chapter 15, there is nothing really special about it at all. Not only so, but we would also be forced to say that a lot of his behaviour was appalling.

In Acts 19:2 twelve religious men declare, 'We have not so much as heard whether there is a Holy Spirit.' If these men had lived at the time of Abraham, there would be nothing unusual in their statement. But as it is, they said it after Pentecost and after the Christian church had existed for many years. Their ignorance was, therefore, a proof that they were unconverted, which explains why Paul treated them as he did.

In Numbers 15:32-36 the Lord instructs that a man found gathering fuel on a Saturday should be executed. I think we need to be very sure where this incident fits on the great storyline, otherwise we may be found applying the Lord's command to his people today, which will result in a massive reduction of people in our churches! Do we need to say any more? The point is clear: no one can be a responsible exegete, and therefore a true preacher of the Word, unless he is crystal clear about the historical setting of the passage that he is about to preach on.

(6) What light do other parts of Scripture shed on this passage?

The Bible, made up of sixty-six books, is a single self-interpreting book. If we find any part of it unclear, other parts will help us to understand it. When we are proudly sure that our interpretation of a particular passage is right, other passages will often correct us and humble us. If we are to be good exegetes, it is essential that we know the whole Bible through and through.

If I were preaching through the Book of Isaiah, I would eventually come to chapter 42. The chapter begins, 'Behold! My Servant whom I uphold . . .'. But who is it speaking about? I do not need to guess. I do not need to be baffled by the wide variety of theories put forward by some of the commentaries. Matthew 12:15-21 tells me that this passage finds its fulfilment in the earthly ministry of the Lord Jesus Christ. Such was his character that he did not provoke unnecessary conflict with his enemies. I can preach a clear message from Isaiah because of the light shed by another part of Scripture.

If I were preaching on Amos 9:11-15 I might be tempted to tell my hearers that the prophet is saying that the Jews will one day have David's descendants restored to them as a royal family, and that in those days the land of Israel will have renewed influence and prosperity. On first sight, that is what the words appear to mean. But we must not rely on first sight. And we must certainly not interpret any passage without asking our sixth question. As it happens, Acts 15:15-17 sheds marvellous light on what Amos says. It shows us that his prediction finds its fulfilment in the conversion of the Gentiles and their becoming part of the Christian church. In doing so, it also gives a key by which we can unlock the meaning of dozens of similar prophecies found in the Old Testament. There can be no exegetical accuracy where there is a failure to interpret Scripture in the light of Scripture.

Who would dare to preach on Melchizedek in Genesis 14:18-24 without referring to Hebrews 5:5-11 and 7:1-28? Who would tell the story of the manna in Exodus chapter 16 without also studying the whole of John chapter 6? Who would try to explain why Dan is missing from the list in Revelation 7:4-8 without tracing the history of that tribe throughout the Old Testament? And who would be bold enough to speak on any doctrinal statement in the Scriptures without keeping in mind all the other passages that treat the same subject? It is vital to compare Scripture with Scripture. If we don't, we will sink into the quicksands of bewilderment, confusion, imbalance and error.

(7) In what way does this passage point to Christ?

We have said something about this in Part One, but it is a point that we cannot stress too much. The Bible is about Christ. He is its great theme. Every single part of it points to him. If I can't see how a particular passage points to him, it is because I have not yet understood that passage as

I should. Where there is no Christo-centricity, there is no exegetical accuracy.

I cannot apologise for what I have just written. All around me are voices which are saying something different. They are proclaiming that it is wrong to insist that the Bible is Christo-centric. That is going too far, they say. According to them we should, rather, say that the Bible is *theocentric*. It is not so much *Christ*-centred as *God*-centred.

With this I agree—and yet I don't agree at all! Yes, of course, I agree that the Bible is a book about God and that it has teaching on God the Father, God the Son and God the Holy Spirit. But this God has no dealings with us *at all* except through Christ. The only God that exists is the God and Father of our Lord Jesus Christ. He has never revealed himself to us except in Christ. There is no way to him except through Christ. The Spirit who works in us is the Spirit of Christ. When we get to heaven the only God we will see is Christ. Nothing, but nothing, can be God-centred unless it is Christ-centred. To think that something can be God-centred without being Christ-centred is a massive error. To admit that the Bible is a book about God is to admit that it is a book about *Christ*!

But each part of the Bible does not point to Christ in exactly the same way. For example, where is Christ in Ecclesiastes? The book tells us that if we leave God out of the picture, life has no meaning, but that it is full of meaning if we love and worship him. But *how* can we know God? Ecclesiastes stirs up this question in our minds but does not give us an answer. It leaves, us hungry to know God, but does not show us the way to him. It is in this way that it points us to Christ. It raises a question to which Christ is the only answer. So it points to him *implicitly*.

Other books of the Bible point to him *explicitly*. This is true of every book in the New Testament. He is mentioned in each one by name. We can also say, then, that these books point to him *directly*. But there are other books in the Scriptures which point to him directly but which do not mention him by name. Isaiah and the book of Psalms would be good examples of this. Other books, such as the first five books of the Bible, for example, point to him by means of predictions, pictures, symbols and ceremonies. We can say that these books speak about him *indirectly*.

Some readers may not be comfortable with the four words that I have just stressed. But I trust that they will agree that the Spirit who inspired every biblical author is the Spirit of Christ. I trust that they will remember that his ministry is always to point to *him*. This is why our Lord could say 'Abraham rejoiced to see my day' (John 8:56), 'Moses . . . wrote about me' (John 5:46) and 'David calls [me] "Lord"' (Matt. 22:45). Every author wrote about the Lord Jesus Christ. Every preacher of those authors should, therefore, preach the Lord Jesus Christ. If Christ is not the sum and the substance of his preaching, he is guilty of exegetical inaccuracy.

How can we help ourselves to be better exegetes?

All this being so, we need to ask ourselves an urgent question: what can we do *concretely* to help ourselves to be better exegetes? No one can exaggerate the importance of this question. Where accurate exegesis dies, preaching dies —and there is no one reading this book who wants that to happen.

There are three things that we can do. If we are not willing to do them, we should stop preaching. Not all of us will be able to do them equally well, but, without exception, all of us are able to make at least some progress in these areas.

(1) We can improve our Bible knowledge

The first thing we can do is to improve our Bible knowledge. This chapter has underlined how important it is to have an intimate and thorough acquaintance with every part of God's written revelation. Every one of us is capable of reading more of the Bible than we are doing at the moment, of asking more questions about what we read, of memorising more key verses and passages, and of taking more time to meditate on the Word of God at different points throughout the day.

Winston Churchill was once beaten by one of his schoolmasters because of his failure to memorise the endings of certain Latin words. In later life he remarked that the only offence for which he would whip a boy was ignorance of his mother tongue. In the same way, we can be lenient with a preacher in all sorts of areas. But we are right to express the deepest disappointment in him if he has anything less than an excellent knowledge of the Bible in his mother tongue.

(2) We can read

No generation of preachers has ever had access to as many books as we do! We can improve our knowledge, and we can improve it *substantially*, in every area where we are lacking. No preacher has any excuse for ignorance about the life and times of any biblical character, of the unfolding of biblical history, of biblical theology, of systematic theology, or of any branch of knowledge useful to the herald of God's Word.

By means of books we can sit at the feet of the greatest teachers that the risen Christ has sent into his church, whether they be living or dead. In addition, those of us who are in the Western world have access to vast resources available to us through recordings, computer programmes and websites. Our Lord said, 'For everyone to whom much is given, from him much will be required; and to whom much has been committed, of him they will ask the more' (Luke 12:48).

It has often been said that there is no real difference between the person who can't read and the person who won't. We live in a busy world. Most of us are under pressure. Many preachers have so many commitments that they can't imagine themselves squeezing in one thing more. But almost all of us, with some thought and rearrangement of our priorities, can find more time to read—we really can! It is time to take ourselves in hand. Our usefulness depends on it. The cause of the gospel requires it.

(3) We can develop skills to help us in understanding the text

There are not many preachers who can learn Hebrew, Aramaic and Greek to a competent level; but some can, and this is one of the reasons why I think that every preacher of the Word should have a go at learning these languages. Most will discover quite quickly that their ability is modest, but at least they will have learned enough to be able to recognise words in commentaries, lexicons and technical books. Almost everyone can learn to use Young's or Strong's concordances, exegetical commentaries, interlinear Bibles, and the countless other lexical aids now available—not forgetting the wonderful computer programmes and internet sites which are ready for use by every serious Bible student.

It is wonderful to live in the twenty-first century. We have access to resources that our forefathers could not even have dreamed of. It is now possible for even the most ordinary preacher to be sure of the grammatical meaning of any part of the Scriptures. He can stand before his congregation and speak with authority from the passage he has opened. But, sadly, in very many places this is not happening. And why is this? It is often because the preacher is lazy, or simply because he has not yet grasped the absolute importance of exegetical accuracy. The aim of this chapter has been to put that right.

* * *

Something to do

1. Write a paragraph about the distinction between exegesis, hermeneutics and exposition, and the intimate connection between them.

2. Mr Smith, a poor exegete, pastored his church for twenty years, and was followed by Mr Jones, a fine exegete, who also pastored there for twenty years. Tell the story of that church during those forty years.

3. Write a letter to a young minister, advising him how to sharpen and maintain his exegetical skills.

2
Doctrinal Substance

WE have seen what preaching is, and we have seen that no one can be a true preacher without committing himself to exegetical accuracy. Nothing can be more important. There is, however, an element in preaching which is second in importance but which is widely neglected today. It is *doctrinal substance*.

What do we mean?

What do we mean by this term? We mean that every sermon we preach should be full of doctrine. It should be rich in theology. The Bible, after all, is a divine revelation. It unveils the mind of God. It reveals to us what we are to believe about him and what he expects of us during our brief lives. Every time the Bible is preached, those who hear it should grow in their understanding of doctrine and duty.

The life expectancy of most of us is between seventy and eighty years. That is plenty of time to read through the Bible several dozen times. A full-time minister who preaches for thirty to forty years also has enough time to exegete it all. And what does the Bible reader, and especially the exegete, discover? He discovers that the Scriptures contain a system of doctrine. With the whole Bible in mind, it is possible to state what it teaches about God, about his decrees, and about creation, providence, redemption, free will, justification, the judgement, heaven and hell, and countless other subjects. People who are weak in systematic theology are, without exception, people who are weak in Bible knowledge.

The fact that the Bible contains a system of doctrine is bound to have an enormous effect on our preaching. Each passage on which I preach, however small it may be, is part of that system and contributes something towards it. This should be brought out during the preaching. That passage, however, does not contain the *whole* of the system, and may well be misunderstood if I do not keep the whole system in mind as I preach. I need the passage, then, to shed light on the system, and I need to draw on the system to shed light on the passage! The current has got to flow in both directions. If it does not, my sermon may well become unbalanced. Who wants to listen to lop-sided sermons? And who wants to preach sermons that can lead people into error?

The Bible is a large box filled with jewels. It is a wonderful thing to pick up each individual jewel, to examine it closely and to be moved by its beauty. But why not also tell people that those gems belong to a King who has a place for each one in his crown? Let them see how all the jewels fit together to adorn the King's head. They will never forget the sight. And never again will they look at each individual jewel as they did before.

The Bible is a glorious garden made up of sixty-six flowerbeds. You, as a preacher, are a guide showing people around. Some guides take the visitors to see one flowerbed at a time. That is good, but there is more to seeing a garden than that. Other guides explain that the different colours and sub-species are found in more beds than one and take their visitors to see all the red flowers, or all the plants in the rose family. That is good, but there is more to seeing a garden than that. Why not also show them that a divine plan has decided the place of each flowerbed and the time of its planting, and that each colour and each flower is part of an enormous and breathtaking pattern? Why not ask them to stand back and see that everything in the garden relates directly to everything else in the garden? Why hide from them the amazing fact that every detail combines together to form a flawless portrait of the Owner?

Let us now put aside our picture language and return more directly to the subject of preaching. This is my firm conviction: if at the end of the sermon my hearers understand the preaching passage, but do not have a better understanding of the *system of truth* that is taught in the Bible, then my preaching is a failure.

I will go further than that. If those who listen to me regularly cannot see that the Bible teaches a system of doctrine and cannot begin to grasp what that system is, I must seriously doubt whether the Head of the Church has ever really sent me to preach 'that form of doctrine' (Rom. 6:17) and 'the pattern of sound words' (2 Tim. 1:13) of which his Word speaks. Yes, preachers whose sermons are without doctrinal substance should give up preaching. The Lord has not sent them.

What happens when preaching is not doctrinally substantial?

To underline the importance of what I have just been saying, let me now show to you what happens when preaching is not doctrinally substantial.

(1) God is not worshipped or loved as he should be

People who have not grasped the system of doctrine contained in the Bible do not know what God is. They do not understand what it means for him to be a Spirit. They do not understand that there are things that can be said about him which cannot be said about any other being. For example, he is infinite, eternal and unchangeable. They do not understand that he is not only infinite, eternal and unchangeable in his being, but in everything he is. As a result, they are not overcome with awe. They do not know what it is for their spirits to go out to him in affectionate trepidation. They do not spend their lives in wonder. There is a whole dimension missing from their spiritual experience.

No other God exists. God is the true God because he is living. And yet, although there is only one God, there are three who are God—God the Father, God the Son and God the Holy Spirit. Each one of these is God in his own right and is God in the same sense. They are distinct, and equal in power and glory. But there are not three gods. The person who knows all this is baffled. He experiences bewildered amazement. He believes what God has declared about himself and bows before the mystery. This, too, is a dimension missing from those who are weak in doctrine.

God has an eternal purpose which depends on nothing except what he has decided within himself. Being God, he orders all events everywhere in such a way that his purpose is served and his name glorified. By his word alone he created from nothing the whole universe to be the stage for these events, and he personally controls everything and everyone on that stage. And so it is that those who are doctrinally instructed study history, read the newspaper, and greet all the joys and heartbreaks of life, in a completely different way to the doctrinally ignorant. They look up to heaven and in everything give thanks.

(2) The Trinitarian nature of salvation is not admired

God's highest and best creation is the human race. What makes us distinct is that we have been made in God's image. It is sad to note that millions of men and women who regularly listen to sermons have no idea what this means. They know little or nothing about the extraordinary dignity they possess and the humility with which they should walk through this world.

The whole of our race is descended from a single pair, and by means of that pair God entered into a covenant with us all. He promised life to those who obey him and death to those who do not. Our first parents chose to disobey and, with one Exception, so have we all. As a result the image of God in us has been defaced, our natures have been irreversibly dirtied and twisted, and we live each day in an ungodly way. We do not enjoy God any more, and we know nothing of the intimate sweetness of walking with him. Instead, we live under his frown and are the objects of his anger. Every setback in life is intended to remind us of this. Meanwhile death waits to reap us and hell waits to burn us.

Those who are doctrinally immature do not weep over the ruin of the human race. They fail to see that our situation is as bad as it really is—a failure which is, of course, a serious sin. They seldom, if ever, think of the ruptured covenant of life and the terrible consequences that affect us all. They do not, then, cry out with relief when they hear of the covenant of grace. In fact, the majority of them do not even know what the covenant of grace is! They have never sung and danced to the music of this doctrine.

As long as God has been God, there are millions of sinners he has loved in a special way. For reasons within himself he decided to rescue them from the pollution and ruin of their disobedient lives and to give them his favour and eternal life. He planned to do this by a Redeemer. This Redeemer is the Lord Jesus Christ, the eternal Son of God, who became a man and who remains the God-Man.

Countless sinners live and die and are damned, but there are some who understand the way to be saved. This is because the Lord Jesus Christ is their *prophet* and, by his Word and Spirit, he reveals this to them. They are filled with sin, but Christ lived a perfect life on their behalf; they deserve to die, but he died for them; they cannot come to God, but he intercedes for them; and all this because he is their *priest*. They cannot believe, but he gives them faith; they cannot remain believing, but he gives them the power; this is because he is their *king*.

From highest glory Christ came to this earth, to the cross and to the tomb. From there he has returned to the highest place of all, a person who is still God but who is also entirely man. He sends the Holy Spirit into the hearts of the millions he has saved, and in this way they actually enter into the experience of salvation. They see their sin and ruin, understand what Christ has done, and entrust themselves entirely to him.

Those who understand Christian doctrine are humbled to know that the Father has always had a special love for them and that he has given them his Son. Warm tears sting their faces as they whisper, 'The Son of God loved me and gave himself for me' (Gal. 2:20). With startled thankfulness they talk of how the Spirit has worked in their lives and brought them to rely on Christ, to personally benefit from his life, death and resurrection. For them, God the Father is their Saviour, God the Son is their Saviour, and God the Holy Spirit is their Saviour. They cannot think about things any other way, and this marks them out from those who have never listened to preaching which is doctrinally substantial.

(3) Believers are unaware of their privileges

Often in Christian meetings and elsewhere men and women give their testimonies. They talk about what they were like before they were converted, how they were saved, and what has happened to them since. You can tell a lot from someone's testimony. You can tell, for example, whether they hear preaching which is doctrinally substantial or not.

When people come to Christ they receive a whole range of blessings right away. They also receive the certainty of receiving even more blessings at death and at the resurrection. Some of the blessings they receive right away are primary blessings, while others are secondary blessings which accompany the primary ones or flow from them. Two of the primary blessings are received in all their fullness, while one of them is received in part, although it is added to day after day.

What *are* the blessings of the Christian life? Which ones come now and which come later? How many primary blessings are there? How many secondary ones? Which of the primary blessings can be described as *acts*, and which one as a *work*? People who listen to doctrinally rich preaching can answer these questions, and they can also give a testimony which is a true reflection of the Christianity found in the Bible. People who are doctrinally deprived can't do either, and their Christian lives are therefore poorer.

The first blessing of the Christian life is *justification*. It is not the highest blessing, but it is the one on which all the other blessings depend. It is something God does. It is an act which flows from his generosity. He pardons all our

59

sins and considers us to be as righteous as he is! This is because all our sins have been put to Christ's account and his spotless righteousness has been credited to our account. We are not justified because of anything at all that we have done, but entirely because of what Christ has done for us. We become justified the very moment we entrust ourselves to the Lord Jesus Christ.

Almost every inward problem that Christians experience is due to the fact that they either forget their justification or do not understand it. Wherever justification is preached and understood you will find believers who are happy and bold, but wherever it is not preached and understood you will find people who are both timid and haunted by un- necessary fears. Most difficulties in our churches would evaporate if justification was understood as it should be. How sad is that church where this great truth is neglected or perverted!

The second great blessing of the Christian life is *adoption*. This is the highest privilege that the gospel offers. It is something God does. It is an act which flows from his generosity. He declares that he is our Father and that we are his sons and heirs, blessed with rights and loaded with privileges. Jesus Christ, his eternal Son, is our Elder Brother. Every other Christian, man or woman, is our brother or sister. A family feeling, given to us by the Holy Spirit, binds us all together. Family duties are also ours; but what care the Father shows for us, and what lib- erty we have in prayer! Christians who do not hear regular doctrinal preaching do not know much about adoption and, I am sad to say, fall easily into joylessness and all sorts of legalism.

The third great blessing of the Christian life is *sanctification*. This is also something God does, but it is a work, not an act. In other words, we do not receive all of this blessing right away. God changes us inside and his image is renewed in us. This inward change means that our behaviour begins to change as well. Little by little, slowly but surely, we sin less and become more and more godly. We work at being like this because God is at work within us. Doctrinal preaching does not only tell us about this wonderful blessing, but also about God's instructions for having a Christlike life.

All sorts of other blessings accompany the three primary blessings and flow from them. For example, we come to have a personal assurance that God loves us. Peace invades our conscience. The Holy Spirit gives us a joy that nothing can take away from us. We become stronger and stronger in our spiritual lives. Despite every obstacle and temptation, we keep on believing until we die.

But what happens at death? Many Christians die in distress because they do not know the answer to this question. Preaching with doctrinal substance would have saved them from the agony of such uncertainty. To play down the place of doctrine in preaching is to be both pastorally insensitive and unkind.

Death is the separation of soul and body. The believer's soul, now sinless, goes immediately and consciously into the presence of Christ, while his body remains Christ's property and waits for the resurrection. The resurrection will be a day of glory for every Christian. He will have a body like Christ's resurrection body. He will be acquitted at the last judgement and welcomed into heaven. He will enjoy God fully, perfectly and for ever. He will be as happy as it is possible to be. Yes, the Christian has a wonderful future. No true preacher could ever be quiet about it.

(4) Believers are confused about how to live

We are looking forward to heaven, but we are still here on earth. As Christian men and women, what should be our great priorities? What principles should govern our daily behaviour? Those who do not hear doctrinal preaching will never know the answer.

As the Lord's people, we have one simple duty: it is to obey God. That is all. It is as straightforward as that. Unfortunately, millions of believing men and women wake up every day and are thoroughly confused about what God expects of them. No clear principle guides them through the day and, as a result, their path is littered with unwise and unhelpful decisions. Again and again they just don't know what to do. They suffer themselves and they frequently bring suffering into the lives of others.

All God has ever wanted is that we should obey him. That was true in the Garden of Eden and it is still true today. Whoever we are, wherever we are, whatever our circumstances, one principle and one principle alone is enough to guide us safely through life: we are to obey God.

So how do we find out what God wants? His Law tells us. That Law consists of the sixty-six books of the Old and New Testaments—nothing more and nothing less. The Bible tells us everything that God expects us to believe and everything that he expects us to do. We need the whole of the Bible, but we do not need anything in addition to the Bible. It is sufficient.

But we have a problem. The average printed Bible contains about 1200 pages and most of us do not know it well or remember it easily. How, then, can we possibly put it into practice in the concrete reality of our daily lives?

God is our heavenly Father and he is filled with tenderness. He has given us a summary of what he expects of us. This summary is called the Ten Commandments. These are made up of ten sentences that God gave to his people in Old Testament times, which our Lord Jesus Christ has stressed are for all his people in all other times. Our Lord was even kind enough to give us a summary of the summary! It goes like this:

'You shall love the LORD your God with all your heart, with all your soul, and with all your mind.' This is the first and great commandment. And the second is like it: 'You shall love your neighbour as yourself.' On these two commandments hang all the Law and the Prophets.

(Matt. 22:37-40)

The Ten Commandments are wonderful. They tell us who our God is, why we should love him, and how we can express that love. They tell us what should go on in our heart, how we should worship, how we should use our tongue and how we should spend our time. They tell us how to honour God in our family and in the community. They teach us to value life, marriage, property and truth. They show us how to be contented in this life and how best to prepare for the next one. They are so simple that almost anyone can remember them easily. They are so profound that even those who have spent their lives studying them continue to be amazed by their wisdom. They crop up in one way or another throughout the Bible and are beautifully fleshed out in the life of Christ. They show us our need of him and find their fulfilment in him.

Christians who listen to doctrinal preaching do not have to grope their way through life. They see the path clearly and walk with their Lord there. They do it with pleasure and not grumpily. And they enjoy marvellous freedom, because their conscience does not feel obliged to do anything except what God specifically requires in his Word. Their happiness and holiness are certainly imperfect, but they are nonetheless a real foretaste of what awaits them in heaven.

(5) Personal witness is impoverished

Where believers do not hear doctrinal preaching, not only are they confused about how to live but also about what to say to unbelievers. As a result, there are not very many Christians who know anything about the joy of soul-winning. All over the world the Lord has his people living among the unconverted, travelling on the same transport as they do, and working alongside them in factories, offices, farms, universities and schools. Most Christians spend their working life in places where no pastor or missionary will ever go. What an opportunity to spread the gospel! But again and again the opportunity is lost because believers don't know what to say.

Like every other Christian, those who are doctrinally instructed face the problem of fear. They are afraid to speak up. But once they do speak up, they are not short of words. They know what message they have got to get across. This is because doctrinal preaching has taught them what unconverted people need to know.

Unconverted people need to be reminded that they know God, although they do not know him as Father and Friend. They may wriggle and protest that this is not true, but the believer must continue to insist that this is the case, and that their wriggling and protesting is an example of how men and women suppress the truth. They are openly denying what their inmost being knows to be a fact. They are not honest. They are guilty of deceit. Their mouths and their hearts contradict each other.

Unconverted people need to be told that their guilt is even greater than this. In their heart they have a sense of right and wrong. They know that God's Law is right, and yet they disobey it in thought, word and action. They do this every day, and so, every day, they infuriate the God who made them and to whom they are answerable. Life is brief, death is certain, and at the last judgement he will call them to account. If they continue to rebel against God, if they continue in their refusing to love him with the whole of their being, they must bear the consequences. He is infinite and eternal. That is the sort of Person they have angered. Justice, therefore, will require a punishment which is also infinite and eternal.

Doctrinally instructed believers are clear about all this. They are clear that this message must be presented with love and concern by people who live Christlike lives, but that it must not be watered down. They are also clear that they must speak to the unconverted about the Lord Jesus Christ. God does not want any sinner to perish. Sinners cannot make up for the past, nor can they save themselves. So God has sent a Saviour who, by his life, death and resurrection, rescues sinners. The doctrinally instructed believer invites, urges and commands them not to turn this Saviour away, but to throw themselves into his care, to entrust themselves to him, and to live under his rule and care.

Unconverted people must repent. They must see their sin, own up to it, be ashamed because of it, and turn from it. They must be thankful for God's kindness and mercy, and must come to Christ, making up their minds to love him and follow him. They must understand that following him means living by his Word, openly associating with his people in a gospel-loving church, and walking with him in prayer.

So it is that the doctrinally instructed Christian does not try to make the gospel message 'user-friendly', although sincere friendliness is part of his personal life. He speaks about sin, guilt, the wrath of God and hell. He speaks about God's kindness, his Son and his willingness to save. He does not hide the fact that no one is saved without repenting. He pleads with people to come to Christ. He shows that coming to Christ is not something that takes place in name only, but that it involves obedience to Scripture, active involvement in the life of his church, and a commitment to prayer.

Those who are doctrinally weak always end up with a message that is not a true reflection of the Bible's message. Their message does not usually start with God. They tend to stress people's need rather than their guilt. They frequently dumb down the issue of repentance. Their presentation of the great saving truths of the gospel is often confusing. They nearly always fail to show that coming to Christ means being committed to a congregation of his people. In short, their message is generally feeble and powerless, rather than robust, demanding, glorious and thrilling. It is little wonder that the true gospel of God is spreading so slowly in the world!

(6) The way to holiness is obscured

Doctrinally ignorant believers are weak in other areas too. In particular, they are not usually very clear about how to become a man or a woman of God. They do not understand how Christians grow. They do not know how to become spiritually strong.

In this twenty-first century we can see examples of this almost everywhere we look. Millions of modern believers have gained the impression that holiness is something you *absorb*. If you can surround yourself with a certain ambience or atmosphere, then something will happen to you. The Lord will draw near to you, you will feel yourself being strengthened, and you will be able to return to your normal life with some sense of spiritual vigour and power.

This way of looking at things largely explains why music has such an important place in many Christian meetings and churches today. Sometimes over half the time that Christians spend together is given over to singing. As the songs continue, people feel increasingly moved and uplifted. They feel that spiritual things are precious to them and that the Lord is meeting with them. They feel that the Holy Spirit is working among them, that the world is unattractive, and that it will be wonderful to be in heaven.

I am writing this as a man who is quite musical and who likes singing the old psalms, as well as any good hymn whether it is traditional or modern. But facts are facts, and we cannot deny them. It is a fact that the New Testament church was not particularly musical and that singing together was not a big part of its life. It is a fact that the church of Jesus Christ spent the first six hundred years of its life without using musical instruments. It is a fact that our Lord's apostles and the Christians of the early church would be quite bewildered by the place given to music if they attended a Christian meeting today.

Doctrinally instructed believers can definitely be music lovers, but they are careful not to give music an important place in their spiritual lives. This is because they know how spiritual growth takes place. It is not something you soak up or absorb. It is not something that just happens to you because of the atmosphere you are in. It may well be expressed in feelings, but it does not *come* to you by means of feelings. It comes to you as the Holy Spirit causes the Scriptures to have an impact on your *mind.*

The Scriptures are the Word of God. This is true, whether we are paying any attention to them or not. Sometimes when they are read, our minds are elsewhere. In those moments the Scriptures have no effect on us and no spiritual growth takes place. But on other occasions the Scriptures strike us. We have some understanding of what they are saying and, at the same time, they stir us and move us. That is not all; we also see that we must put them into practice. *This* is when we are spiritually strengthened.

It is the Lord's will that the Scriptures should be read publicly when his people meet together. This is even more important than reading the Bible on our own. How can I say such a thing? It is because God did not give his Word to individuals, but to his *church*; and the Bible is most blessed and best understood when his people gather round it together.

However, the public reading of Scripture is not enough. Our Lord Jesus Christ, seated at his Father's right hand, sends into his church a stream of men whom he has equipped to teach the Bible to his people. Just as preaching is the chief means by which sinners are convinced of gospel truth and are converted, in the same way it is God's chief way of building up his people in holiness, of comforting them, and of keeping them believing until the end of their lives. No Christian can grow as he should without listening to lots of preaching. It is an impossibility. It is this fact, of course, which requires preachers to do their job well—which explains why this little book on preaching is more important than some people might think.

Doctrinally instructed Christians know all this, and they also know that preaching must be listened to in a certain way. Preaching is so vitally necessary to our spiritual strength that we must make every effort to hear it regularly. Before we hear it, we need to prepare our hearts and to pray for the preacher. During the sermon we must reject what is false, and believe and love what is true. When it is over, we need to take the time and trouble to call it to mind, and then to see that we put it all into practice. This is the way to spiritual growth. This is how God gives us a Christlike character.

(7) Church life is not ordered

But there is more to church life than gathering with other believers to listen to sermons. This is the church's most important activity, but it is not its only activity, as sermons from the Word of God will inevitably make clear!

Doctrinally instructed Christians understand about church life. They know that when people claim to have repented and to have put their trust in the Lord Jesus Christ, that claim should be examined. The people best placed to examine that claim are the spiritually mature men who make up the leadership of a Christ-loving, Bible-believing Christian congregation. If the claim seems to be well-founded, the new convert is to be baptised and admitted into the fellowship of that congregation.

It is only in such a context that a new Christian can be properly nurtured. The local church welcomes him or her as a new brother or sister in the faith. It provides love, under-standing, support, practical help, teaching, restorative discipline, and everything else that a new believer might need. It is by persevering in the faith in the context of a local church that we give the proof that we are indeed new people in Christ and members of that true church which includes all believers in all places in all generations.

A fairly regular highlight in local church life is the Lord's Supper. It is Christ's will that our spiritual lives should not only be strengthened by his Word and by prayer, but also by his sacraments. Some people don't like the word 'sacrament', but a better word has never been found. Baptism is the first sacrament and the Lord's Supper is the second. Neither of these acts can do us any good unless Christ himself blesses them and his Spirit works through them. They are moving pictures which teach us about Christ and his gospel, which give us a fuller appreciation of what he has done for us, and which strengthen our faith in him and our enjoyment of him.

As Christians we are baptised one at a time, and this happens to us only once. Baptism is our badge of discipleship. It is done in the name of the Father and of the Son and of the Holy Spirit, to show that we now have the Triune God as our Saviour and Lord, and that we owe our salvation entirely to his grace and not to anything in ourselves.

The Lord's Supper is different. It is something we enjoy together as church members, and which we do regularly throughout our lives. In the way that Christ has appointed, we eat bread together and then drink wine together. The bread represents Christ's body and the wine represents his blood, and by our eating and drinking we both remember and proclaim his death. As we do so (as long as we are conscious of what we are doing), our hearts connect with his and we are nourished and strengthened spiritually. Our hearts also connect with

70

each other in loving fellowship. The Bible teaches that what goes on inside us is actually more important than the outward ceremony and symbols, because if our heart is not *in* what we are doing, the whole experience is certain to be spiritually damaging.

What has all this to do with preaching? We are continuing to make the point that preaching must have doctrinal substance, and that preaching which lacks it robs its hearers of countless benefits. Millions of believers limp along in spiritual weakness because they have never understood that it is impossible to make any real spiritual progress without being members of a gospel church. How many people are there who claim to be Christians, but who have never had their claim examined by anyone except themselves? How many professed believers are there who have never been baptised and who live their lives in open disobedience to Christ by not becoming committed to a Bible-centred congregation?

How many are there who regard attendance at the Lord's Supper as something you can miss without holding back your spiritual development? Who can count the number of Christians who actually believe that it is more important to read the Bible on your own than to have it preached to you? Where are the believers who are bold enough to flag up the Bible's teaching that the local church is the *only* suitable place for a young Christian to be nurtured? What shall we say about the almost universal abandonment of loving church discipline, despite the fact that it is an ordinance of Christ? And will we ever hear the end of the lie that says someone's claim to be a member of Christ's church can be taken seriously even when that person has no commitment to a local Christian congregation?

71

What can be done? Can anything sort out this mess? Yes, one thing, and one thing only—a return to preaching which is doctrinally substantial!

(8) Prayer is superficial

We cannot close this chapter without saying something more about prayer. Every Christian in the world will tell you that it is important. Most of them will tell you that we start the Christian life with prayer and that we need it every day afterwards. But what actually *is* it? This is the question which causes many of them to hesitate, because they know that their answer is neither clear nor complete.

The doctrinally instructed Christian has no such problem. He knows that prayer is not a matter of words, although it may be expressed in words. Prayer is a matter of the heart. It is the heart making its desires known to God. Its chief desire is that God will only grant what *he* desires.

The Christian heart knows that it has no entry into God's presence except through Christ, and so, as it makes its desires known to God, it relies entirely on Christ. It also knows that the only thing that hinders communion with God is sin, so it is quick to confess every sin that it knows about. In addition, it does not see prayer as simply making requests; it has an earnest desire to thank God for every display of his goodness.

As the desires flow from the praying heart to God, they do not surge out as an uncontrolled flood, because there is one desire which rules all the others; it is the desire to obey God. Spiritually-minded people know that God does not want them to pray in a jumbled and untidy manner. This is because he has given us many examples of prayer in his

Word, but supremely because his Son has told his disciples how to pray. The Lord's Prayer is to be our model. Architects do not build models in order to live in them, but to use them as the basis of their constructions; in the same way the praying heart is not satisfied by reciting the Lord's Prayer, but uses it to organise the desires which spring from its inmost being.

It is rare, then, that true prayer is addressed to Jesus or to the Spirit. It comes with dependence, love and awe to the Father. It thinks great thoughts about him and desires that others should do the same. It asks that evil may be thrown down, that his kingdom may spread in the world, and that his final kingdom will come shortly. It longs that the church on earth may be as obedient to him as the elect angels in heaven. It requests that every member of Christ's church may have their daily needs supplied. In deep consciousness of its sin, it pleads for forgiveness, but only on the condition that it is ruled by a forgiving spirit itself. It shudders at the thought of sin, cries out to be spared temptation and begs never to fall into the devil's power. It breathes with relief that God is the eternal King and that it has spoken to no one else but him.

Very few modern Christian are giants in prayer. Prayers spoken in our meetings are very often shallow, banal, repetitive, and even heretical. We rarely hear anything that follows the biblical pattern, bringing us to engage with God, and leaving us thrilled, humbled and ennobled. What has happened? Has true prayer left us for ever? Can anything, anything at all, change the situation?

True biblical preaching can change the situation. Such preaching is not only exegetically accurate but also doctrinally substantial. If God blesses it, it will heal all the distresses and put right all the errors that we have mentioned in this chapter. Non-doctrinal preaching is ruining the church. We cannot allow things to go on as they are. We must turn things round and, with God's help, we will—by a return to unashamed, heartfelt, Christ-centred, doctrinal substance.

* * *

Something to do

1. 'Without theology there is no preaching, at least in the New Testament sense' (Donald MacLeod).[1] Discuss this statement.

2. Give the outline of a sermon you might preach on 1 Samuel chapter 3, and list the doctrinal teaching you could include in it.

3. Make practical suggestions as to how all the major doctrines of the faith could be taught to an average congregation.

[1] 'Preaching and Systematic Theology' by Donald MacLeod (chapter 19 in *Preaching*, ed. Samuel T. Logan (Welwyn, Evangelical Press, 1986), p. 246.

3
Clear Structure

We have learned what preaching is. We have also learned that our preaching must be characterised by exegetical accuracy and doctrinal substance. But all our hard work will be wasted, and all our opportunities will be lost, if our hearers cannot follow us when we speak and cannot remember afterwards what we have said. The good news is that this does not need to happen. Our sermons will be both easy to follow and easy to remember if they always have a *clear structure*.

Preachers who love their people are fussy about the structure of their sermons. They know that the most ordinary person will never lose their way, as long as the sermon has unity, order and proportion. *Unity* means that the message all holds together; it is not made up of several disconnected sermonettes. *Order* means that the sermon is made of distinct ideas which follow each other in a logical chain that leads up to a climax. *Proportion* means that each idea is given its proper place; unimportant things are not magnified, and important things are not played down. The worst preacher on earth will improve immediately if he remembers these three words.

I have often been told that 'order is heaven's first law'. Certainly God is a God of order. Anyone who has ever reflected on the Holy Trinity knows that there is an order and symmetry within the being of God which is breathtaking in its beauty. Disorder is another word for ungodliness.

75

For many years I lectured on preaching in a theological college, or, as it is called in North America, a seminary. My students were men who were training for the pastoral ministry and for cross-cultural missionary work. All of them wanted to be compelling preachers. But I knew that some of them were unlikely to make it, and on this point I was seldom wrong. This is because I had visited them in their student accommodation or in their homes.

Let me tell you about a student that I will call Frank. Every time I visited him in his student residence, he was neatly dressed and working at an uncluttered desk in a clean and tidy room. His clothes were neatly folded in their drawers or hanging in his wardrobe. Order was important to Frank, and yet his neatness was nothing like that fanatical tidiness which makes visitors uncomfortable. Order was in his *soul*. I therefore expected that he would develop into a fine preacher, which in fact has proved to be the case. He preaches appealing and powerful sermons where the ideas follow each other in an attractive logic that even children can follow without effort. His people love him and his usefulness increases from year to year.

I will call another student George, and he stands in complete contrast to Frank. George's room really did look as if a bomb had hit it! It was never clean. The floor was covered with clothes, cups, books and pieces of paper. His desk was piled with clutter, so he did most of his study sitting on a bed that was a jungle of disarray. He did not value order. It was not part of his life. As a result, it was not part of his preaching. What he said was good, but his ideas were not organised. Out of his mouth came a jumble of treasures that tumbled into each other in a way that left people's heads clanging in confusion. After preaching so badly for so long, I am glad to tell you that George is now making some progress—but only because he is *at last* beginning to see the importance of clear structure.

Clear structure means that each sermon we preach will have an introduction, something to say (traditionally called 'the discussion'), and a conclusion. We will now look at these three elements in turn.

[1] The introduction

Definition

The introduction is composed of the opening remarks which prepare the audience for everything that follows. This chapter has opened with an introduction! The introduction is the porch that welcomes you into the house, the dawn that precedes the sunrise, the prelude that makes you want to hear the symphony, and the hors d'oeuvres that stimulate your appetite before your meal.

Purpose

The introduction has only one purpose: it sets out to get people interested in the subject you are going to speak about. When we stand up to preach, we have all sorts of people in front of us and all sorts of obstacles to overcome. One obstacle is *apathy*; the person is not interested in anything that is going on. Another is *antipathy*; the person is actually against us and what we stand for. Yet another is *incredulity*; the person does not believe the Book we are about to preach from. Somehow or other, we have got to get every person present ready to listen to what we have to say. We have got to overcome inertia, to arouse attention, to excite interest and to prepare the way. We have got to get people from where they are to the point where they will give us a ready hearing.

'What is the best way to get the attention of the congregation?' once asked a young preacher. 'Give 'em something to attend to!' replied the old saint.

A story from long ago tells us of a Russian peasant who had a particularly stubborn donkey. It only obeyed its master when it felt like it, which was quite a rare event! But the peasant heard of a doctor who claimed that he had a painless method of training donkeys to be obedient, so he pleaded with him to come to his farm. On seeing the donkey, the doctor took a large wooden club out of his bag and began mercilessly beating the animal all over his head. 'Stop! Stop!' cried the peasant, 'You told me that your training method was painless!' 'So it is', replied the doctor, 'But I have got to get his attention first!'

It is easy to preach to an audience that is giving us its attention and is also interested in what we are going to say. 'Well begun, half done', says the old proverb.

Suggestions

The introduction should lead directly into the discussion. It is not a sidetrack. It is a slip road that goes nowhere except on to the motorway. Everything in the introduction should serve this one purpose.

The introduction should not promise more than the sermon can supply. Some introductions are so good that the sermon which follows is an anticlimax. If the porch is impressive, we expect the house behind it to be even more impressive. It is always a disappointment to walk through a beautiful porch into a rickety shed!

The introduction should contain a single thought. It should be simple and modest. Who wants to walk through a porch into another porch, which in turn leads into another porch?

It is important to vary our introductions. I have spent a major part of my life living in a terraced house in the inner city. In a terraced street, dozens of houses join on to each other. They all look the same. But even in this situation some variety is possible. At least each house can have a different colour for its front door!

It should not be too long. Mr Smith, a businessman, has arrived early for an important meeting. He sits on a chair in the corridor and falls asleep. A little later a secretary taps him on his arm and guides him into the meeting room, where she leaves him and his colleagues to get on with their business. Her name is Mrs Introduction.

The introduction introduces people to the main business of the day, but it is *not* that main business. Its aim is to wake people up and to prepare them for what follows. Its aim is certainly not to wake people up and then to drive them to sleep again, and it must take care to avoid confusing or misleading them before they get to the big truths that are about to be explained.

A long introduction is always a fault. A short one seldom is. We must not spend so long laying the tablecloth that people wonder whether they are ever going to get any dinner!

How carefully, then, it must be prepared! We are going to arrest people! We must think out what our opening remarks will be, and inexperienced preachers should perhaps also write them out. So let's put ourselves in our hearers' shoes and work out how we are going to grab their attention. If we see people sit up and look straight at us, we will know that we have succeeded.

Sources

As I try to improve my introductions, where can I get some good ideas? Books on preaching usually have a great deal to say about this. My own conviction is that we all need to know our hearers as well as we can, and then to use some flair and originality in the way that we capture them. As quickly and as attractively as possible, we want to get them to be enthusiastic about our subject, always remembering that the truth which is to follow must be infinitely more glorious than the introduction which precedes it. I have no magic formula. Good introductions are the result of thought, prayer, and love for our people. Where these three elements are present we will seldom do badly.

[2] The discussion

Definition
The introduction is followed by what has been traditionally called 'the discussion'. But what is that? It is the truth to be taught to *these* people *now*. It is composed of the material that I have set myself to get across in this particular sermon.

A plan essential
To get this truth across effectively, I must have a plan. After all, I am going to be teaching people *truth*. My thoughts must follow each other in some sort of prearranged order, or I will get nowhere. People must sense that there is some movement in the sermon which is leading them in a definite direction.

The plan of the sermon should be as simple as possible so that every hearer can see where they are going. It is difficult to drive on a dark road at night. But if there are Catseyes in the middle of the road, everything is easier. As the headlights shine, the reflective studs come into view one at a time. We have plenty of notice before we come to any twist or turn.

Although the plan should be simple, it should also be both fresh and striking. If it isn't, the congregation will switch off. Every heart will groan to itself, 'I can see what's coming.' And yet the plan must not be smart, or odd or clever. We need a memorable structure which will not cause people to either admire us or despise us, but which will fix their eyes firmly on the truth we are presenting.

It is time to abandon all sermon plans that are difficult, stiff, monotonous or boring, as well as those that are brilliant and breathtaking. It is *God*'s truth that we are preaching! Nothing must make it difficult to grasp, or divert people's attention from it. Our reason for having a plan springs from our burning ambition that every person should have no problem in seeing what God's truth is.

The helpfulness of divisions

In order to keep us to our plan, and to help our hearers see what it is, a sermon should have distinct divisions, or headings. These act like snow poles on a winter road. When the snow is deep, the driver cannot see where the road is. It is easy for him to wander off it and to become completely lost. Brightly coloured poles marking the edges of the road are all that he needs. If these are in place, he is completely safe.

Divisions, or headings, make the sermon easy to follow. Our hearers can see the argument develop. They can see where they have been and where they are going next. We must not forget that men and women were originally made in God's image. That image has been horribly distorted and spoiled, but it is still present. The result is that the human mind does not take kindly to disorder and chaos. Sermons without divisions are likely to dehumanise people.

Divisions also make the sermon easy to remember. How can our preaching do any lasting good if our hearers cannot recall it? Each heading acts like a peg on which people can hang a newly learned truth. When all the pegs are in mind, they cannot only recall the whole sermon, but they can better understand how one truth relates to another.

Some rules about divisions

However, divisions or headings cease to be useful if they are not done well. We will structure our sermons helpfully enough if our divisions fit the following description:

Distinct

Each heading must be distinct from all the others and not a rehash of any of them. It must have its own obvious identity. In this way our hearers will see that the sermon has progression. They will see that each division is building on the previous one and leading to the next one. Each heading is distinct because it has a unique place in the argument.

Orderly, moving, progressing

A merry-go-round at the fun park has order and movement, but it makes no progress. Who wants to listen to a sermon like that? A rioting mob has movement and progress, but it has no order. Who in his right mind would be happy with a sermon like that? But an army on the move has all three characteristics. It gets somewhere and it does something. Is there any need to say anything more?

Cumulative

A falling object gets faster and faster as it falls. Because of its pent-up energy, even a golf ball could kill somebody if it was dropped from a height. A sermon should gather strength as it proceeds, and this gathering strength should be expressed in its headings. It should be plain to all that the argument is moving along and that it is gathering force. The divisions should lead into each other quite naturally and in a way that makes sure that the current of thought is channelled, rather than lost. Each division should make the hearers more and more keyed up about the coming climax.

Comprehensive

Before he begins to speak, the preacher should be entirely clear about exactly how much truth he intends to get across. In all normal circumstances he should stick to that and not give anything more, except by way of further explanation, illustration or application. His headings should provide a complete and concise summary of the truth he has covered. They should squeeze out of the orange all the juice that he wants to give, but not a drop more.

Natural

The headings should be natural and not forced. In his preparation the preacher must always ask how his verse, or passage, or theme, divides up naturally. Nothing must be imposed upon it which is not already there. Headings are levers which prise out treasures from the ground; they are not vehicles which import them from elsewhere.

Few

A sermon should not have too many divisions. When I was a boy, it was still legal to take eggs from the nests of certain birds. Bird-nesting was a favourite occupation of many children who lived in the country, and in our family we had quite a good collection. If we brought an egg home, my parents always wanted to know how many eggs had been in the nest. If there were more than four, they were content. Like many other people, they held to the theory that a bird could only count up to four! It would therefore not miss the egg that had been stolen and would not suffer any distress!

I don't know if this old theory is correct or not. But I do know that people find it hard to follow or retain a sermon that has more than four points. If there are only two points, it is hard to keep people's interest, to have progression in the sermon, and to introduce much in the way of variety. If there are too many points, the sermon becomes extremely difficult to remember. This is why it is wise to have three points (despite all the teasing that goes on about this!), or a maximum of four.

A sermon with three or four divisions avoids almost every danger. The simplest form of logic, the syllogism, has three points. An example of a syllogism goes like this:

- All postmen wear blue trousers.
- John is a postman.
- Therefore John wears blue trousers.

With three points, therefore, it is possible not only to have plenty of variety, but also to have a logical argument leading to a climax or conclusion. We should stop laughing about preachers who have three divisions. Three-point sermons have been a very good teaching tool through the centuries. Again and again, they have been wonderfully used in making God's truth clear.

Proportionate
As a general rule, each division in a sermon should be of about the same length. Recently I heard a young preacher

whose message had three clear points. He spent twenty-three minutes on the first point, seven on the second, but only three on the third! The impression he left was that he had spent too much time on his first division, and that he had short-changed us on the other two. We felt that the sermon had been unbalanced, but also, mysteriously, that we had been cheated. No preacher should leave this sort of impression; people ought to leave church moved, thrilled and subdued by the Word of God. The structure is there to serve the Word, not to distract from it.

Persuasive

If we think carefully about our headings, we can place them in a way that makes them more persuasive. In Matthew 6:1-18 our Lord teaches his disciples about charitable deeds, prayer, and fasting. On each occasion he tells them what *not* to do before he tells them what they *should* do. This is a good example to follow; negative should precede positive. In the same way, abstract should come before concrete, false before true, and statement before appeal or exhortation. Why rob our messages of force when, by a little thought and rearrangement, we can make them more convincing?

Attractive

In the same way, by taking time to think things through, we can make our headings more attractive. After all, aren't we longing that our sermons should be interesting, easy to follow, and even easier to remember? We will make immediate progress just by simplifying our words—'three blind mice' makes much more sense to people than 'a tertiary number of visually impaired rodents'! A heading expressed in a single word always carries more weight than one expressed in a long phrase—'wow!' is more memorable than 'the elation we should feel and express'! And why do headings have to be expressed in statements? Wouldn't it be much more arresting to express them as questions? Couldn't all of us, with prayer and care, present our divisions more attractively?

[3] The conclusion

All good things come to an end, and so do all sermons, good or bad. But what is the best way of bringing them to a close? What makes a helpful conclusion? Those who are interested in sermon structure are never willing to duck such questions as these.

Definition
The conclusion is composed of the remarks that close the sermon. Its aim is to round off the message in a way that is worthy of the truths that have been preached. It also seeks to make sure that nothing important is lost, but that it remains imprinted on the minds and consciences of every person present.

Some years ago my wife and I were surprised to find a small chocolate factory hidden away in a North Wales village. The owner was a Swiss *chocolatier* who made each individual chocolate by hand. This, of course, meant that his products were extremely expensive. Because he had been so kind to us, and because we had found our tour of his factory so interesting, we decided to buy six of his chocolates. He treated each one with almost fatherly affection as he placed them in a brightly coloured bag, which he then tied up with string and entrusted to our care. He was as anxious as we were that not one of them should be lost on the way home. His care and that bag were a fitting conclusion to our visit.

Importance

The conclusion is capable of increasing the sermon's usefulness, but it is equally capable of ruining it. It can drive the truth home, but it can also drive it away. It can print it in every hearer's heart or it can smudge it beyond recognition. The last few sentences of the sermon have an importance that no one can exaggerate.

What is the point of preaching a rousing sermon if its last few minutes bore everyone silly? If a sermon wakes people up, but ends by sending them to sleep, what possible good can it do? If the teaching is as clear as can be, but the conclusion is vague or confusing, what lasting benefit can it possibly carry?

As a child I was taught to make sugar candy. Vast quantities of sugar were poured into boiling water, which was then left to cool. As it did so, the dissolved sugar began to crystallise around strings which had been left dangling in the water. Those delicious lumps of sweetness are like good conclusions—everything in the sermon crystallises into a form which can easily be carried away.

We know, though, that not everything in a sermon is likely to be sweet. Perhaps it would be better to compare the conclusion to the point of an arrow. It is propelled quickly into the air by a bowstring (the introduction) and kept on course by three or four feathers called flights (the divisions), but its work is not done until it strikes its target. At that moment its whole force is concentrated into its point, and it is that point that penetrates the target. A blunt arrow hits the target and falls to the ground. It accomplishes nothing at all. What a waste! Everything would have been different if the end of the arrow had been sharpened.

Suggestions
Sharpen the arrow! Carefully prepare your sermon's conclusion! Write down *precisely* what you want to leave ringing in people's ears and either commit it to memory or include it (in full) in your notes.

We should prepare our conclusion before we prepare the final version of our message. It should be in our mind at every point. Every weapon that we bring out from our armoury should be one that serves that conclusion. We must never lose sight of it. At every point we should be perfectly clear about where we want this sermon to end up.

I am a man who believes that church buildings should be simple and without ornament. But let us pretend for a moment that I am an architect who is designing an impressive church building with a spire. That spire would be in my mind from the very beginning. It is the feature I would want everyone to see. It would figure in every drawing and would dominate all my plans. But at what point in the construction would it be built? In the same way, a sermon's conclusion is first in conception but last in execution.

The conclusion should be short. The discussion is over and it is not right to start it all over again. It is time to drive it home! It is true that the conclusion should be long enough to honour the discussion that has preceded it. But we must remember that its purpose is to conclude!

Our conclusions should be varied. If they are not, our regular hearers will quickly see what is coming and there will be no element of surprise. They will begin to shuffle and to pick up their hymn books before we have finished. I am glad that I spent my student years under the powerful ministry of Paul Tucker in East London Tabernacle. His sermons were not lengthy, but it was impossible to guess when he was going to finish. Suddenly he would gather up everything he had said and would thrust it with affectionate authority into our hearts and lives. We never saw it coming. He held us spellbound until the last moment. But we never left the building without hearing ringing words that both encapsulated the message and told us what to do with it.

There are not many men today who preach like Mr Tucker. It seems to me that countless preachers must study within earshot of a spin-dryer. Everything is going at full speed but then, almost unnoticeably at first, things begin to slow down. After that they get slower and lower, slower and lower, until they come to a dead stop. The congregation looks up with uncertainty; is this the end, or is he going to start up again? That is the only moment of suspense that they ever feel! Such boring endings do nothing to command respect for the truth that has just been preached.

Our conclusions should be pointed and personal. The whole purpose in preaching God's Word is that people should be changed by it. The conclusion must demand a verdict from *him* and *him* and *her* and *her*. Each person must understand that they are now faced with a choice— they must now put what they have heard into practice, or they must refuse to do that. They cannot remain neutral. God's truth demands a personal response. Truths must be enjoyed, promises must be believed, privileges must be entered into, comforts must be embraced, duties must be fulfilled, sins must be forsaken and warnings must be taken seriously—or they must all be thrown away. But no one can remain as they are. A decision must be made *right now*. The conclusion must insist on this. And then it must stop.

* * *

A tale of two sitting rooms

We have now covered all that needs to be said about clear structure, so please let me finish with a tale of two sitting rooms.

Last Sunday Mrs McGregor went to church. The sermon was exegetically accurate and filled with wholesome doctrine, but it didn't do her any good whatever. Nor could she tell her unconverted husband much about it when she got home, although he seemed quite interested to know what she had heard. So what was the problem? The fact is that the message was a string of sentences that had little or no structure, at least as far as she could tell. So she could not follow it, she could not retain it, and she could not talk about it. How was God glorified by that?

Last Sunday John Jones went to church. The sermon was exegetically accurate and filled with wholesome doctrine. He couldn't wait to get home. He bounded up the stairs two at a time and told his invalid wife all about it. He could remember it so easily that he took her through it point by point; in fact he almost preached it to her! She, in turn, was thrilled, moved and helped. In that upstairs sitting room two hearts went out afresh to the Lord.

For the sake of God, and for the good of those who hear us, whether they be converted or unconverted, let us give ourselves to mastering the skill of preaching with clear structure!

* * *

Something to do

1. You are having Sunday lunch with a Christian family which is discussing the structureless sermon preached that morning. Write down what you might hear.

2. Suggest an extended outline for a sermon on Romans 12:1-2 and justify your structure.

3. Some people argue that as the Holy Spirit is the Divine Instructor, and he alone makes the things of God plain, there is no need whatever to be concerned about a sermon's structure. Write down what you think about such an opinion.

4
Vivid Illustration

It must now be clear to us that good preaching requires a lot of work beforehand. But all our labours will be lost if our preaching cannot be followed or remembered. It was for that reason that we spent a chapter looking at the question of clear structure. The same reason now drives us to the subject of *vivid illustration*.

[1] The value of illustrations

An illustration is a word-picture that sheds light, or lustre, on something. It is a window which lets light into a dark room. Many people today are not very good with words. They find abstract logic and theoretical reasoning very hard to cope with. Deep, sustained arguments leave them bewildered. When words are used in these ways, they feel like people lost at night. Won't somebody help them to see? Doesn't anyone have a pair of infra-red goggles or, even better, a bright torch?

Most people cannot understand anything very well unless they can see it in their minds. They respond well to words which project pictures, but consider words on their own to be dull, boring and uninteresting. *The Archers* is a British radio programme that has been broadcast almost every day for over fifty years. Millions of people still listen to it. They hear the actors speak their words, but there is nothing at all to see. So what is the appeal of this programme? It advertises itself as 'an everyday story of country folk'. Its fans do not tune in to a torrent of abstract propositions, but to a story that they can see unfolding in their minds.

Many preachers are very critical of modern culture, and especially of its dependence on word-pictures. I am asking them to face up to the facts. They may not like the way things are, but they must remember that it is to *this* generation that the Lord has called us to preach, and this generation is one that needs word-pictures. Besides, what is so awful about that? The Scriptures contain such pictures on every page, and our Lord used them all the time.

The question of illustration demands our urgent attention. We must stop being like broadcasters who try to comment on football games where the floodlights have been switched off. Put the lights on! Display the Word in all its colour and movement. Work on your illustrations and, to see their value, consider the following three points:

(i) They explain the truth
This is why our Lord so often said, 'The kingdom of heaven is like . . .' (e.g. Matt. 13:24,31,33,44,45,47). Once a word-picture is lodged in a person's mind, everything becomes plain.

In Romans chapters 6 and 7 the apostle Paul is trying to explain why it is absurd for people who are justified by faith to continue living in sin. I, for one, would find those chapters difficult to understand if they were filled with complex and closely reasoned arguments. But they are not. Paul talks about a slave who dies to one master, but who is resurrected to serve another. He talks about a slave market where you can tell which slave belongs to which master. He talks about a marriage where one spouse dies and the other is freed to marry someone else. The apostle uses nothing but words, and yet he talks to us in pictures. Not only do his pictures help us to understand, but they also convince us of what he is saying. Shouldn't we copy the apostle's example? Does anyone know of a better way of explaining truth?

(ii) They make the truth attractive

Have you ever watched a preacher losing his congregation? People are not leaving the room, but it is clear that their thoughts are elsewhere. Suddenly they sit up, look at the preacher and give him their full attention. What is happening? What has made the difference? He is using an illustration!

Preachers cannot always make things easy. Some things in the Bible are hard to understand. But people can only listen to difficult things for a limited amount of time. Give them a rest, give them some refreshment, and very quickly they will be ready to listen to you again.

Most people in Switzerland do not live in chalets but in blocks of flats. Almost every block of flats has a lift and—wonder of wonders!—these lifts hardly ever break down. If they do, you can always use the stairs. There are two flights of stairs for every floor, and where they meet there is almost always a chair! It is difficult climbing up stairs, but if you take your time and rest on each chair, you will find that it is not so difficult after all. Illustrations in a sermon are like those chairs.

If we have to go on a long journey in a limited amount of time, most of us will choose to drive on the motorway. It is not nearly so interesting as driving along country roads. Every mile seems very similar to the previous one. After a while we get tired of it all and decide to stop at the motorway services. We go to the toilet, have a cup of tea and spend a few minutes in the shop. At this point we find that we are not only ready to go again, but that we are eager to do it! What has happened to us? We have been rested and refreshed. Illustrations in sermons are like those motorway stops.

Have you ever read a story to a young child who is sitting beside you? At first he is interested and amused, but after a little while he begins to fidget. Then everything changes and he is urging you to go on. You have turned the page and he has seen a picture!

Because they make the truth attractive, illustrations also make it impressive. Our Lord could have said something like this: 'Whatever you have done, however long you have been doing it, wherever it has taken you, if you turn back to God, he will welcome you.' But he didn't. He said, rather, 'A certain man had two sons . . .' (Luke 15:11). The parable of the Prodigal Son impresses the Father's welcome on us in a way that no mere statement could ever hope to do. We see the truth, we see it clearly, and we weep for joy.

When David sinned so brazenly against the Lord, and then followed his adultery and murder with months of prayerlessness, God sent the prophet Nathan to him. Did Nathan storm into the king's presence, point the finger in holy rage and denounce him? He was too wise for that. His aim was to restore the fallen sinner, not to drive him to apostasy. He entered gently and told a story. Very soon it was the king, not the prophet, who was in a rage. But three thousand years later we are still struck by the authority of Nathan's 'You are the man!' (2 Samuel 12:7).

(iii) They make the truth memorable
What can you remember about the last sermon you heard? Did it have a few striking sound bites? Were there some

impressive flights of speech? Were there some brilliant examples of persuasive argument? Are these the things you remember? Probably not. But I am sure that you, like me, can remember the illustrations!

Many years ago, right at the beginning of my ministry, I was given a special invitation to attend the post-mortem examination of a smoker. The idea was that I should be so shocked at what tobacco smoking does to people's lungs that I would use my influence as a minister to discourage smoking everywhere. I am a squeamish man and I would probably have fainted if I had attended. So I turned down the invitation. But of one thing I am sure: if I had accepted, I would have been infinitely more impressed by what I saw than by all the statistics about smoking I have ever read. We remember what we see. We forget most of what we read and hear.

As preachers, we do not use visual aids. Our Lord has called us to work with words. But we are to use those words to stimulate people's God-given power of imagination. We are to put eyes into people's ears. There is no better way to reach their minds.

When we stand up to preach, we have all sorts of people in front of us. They vary in ethnicity, age, background, education, skill, knowledge, temperament, character, and a good deal else besides. But we can catch them *all* with a thoughtful illustration. This is what our Lord did with his parables, and especially with the parables he taught during the days leading up to his crucifixion. An excellent example is the parable of the wicked vine-dressers found in Mark 12:1-12, as well as the three parables in Matthew chapter 25. During this period our Lord spoke to a wider variety of people than normal. His audience included highly educated enemies who were not normally present during his ministry out of Jerusalem. He taught them uncomfortable truths that they would never forget!

A *remembered* truth may do its work long, long after the sermon has been given. In my twenties I read several sermons by F. B. Meyer. They contained illustrations which have helped me in my Christian life right up to this very day. In the same way, my soul continues to feed on the sermons of Hywel Griffiths of Bridgend, who was undoubtedly the greatest preacher I have ever heard. I was twenty years old when I first heard him on one of his annual visits to our small village in South Pembrokeshire, and his preaching on those occasions does me good almost every day. This is not because I have any recordings; it is simply that I *remember* them. I have heard thousands of sermons through the years and almost all of them have no place in my memory. But the preaching of Hywel Griffiths lives on, first of all because of its heavenly power (a subject we will return to in another chapter), and secondly because his preaching was illustrative from beginning to end.

What people see, they remember. What people see in their *minds*, they also remember. That is the way we are built. People who have not been near a church for forty years, but who went to Sunday school during their childhood, can still remember a dozen Bible stories. People who know almost nothing worthwhile about British history can nonetheless often tell you about King Alfred and the cakes, the death of King Harold at the Battle of Hastings, and Sir Francis Drake continuing to play bowls despite the approach of the Spanish Armada! Can we not then use more illustrations in our preaching and help them to remember the *gospel*?

A book that has done a lot to shape my own views on preaching is *Some Great Preachers of Wales* by Owen

Jones.[1] This book has a close look at several men whose powerful preaching resulted in the conversion of thousands, and who consequently transformed the nation. The most helpful part of the book is its introductory essay, in which Mr Jones identifies five characteristics that these preachers had in common. It is interesting to note that one of them was *imagination*! These men, in different measures, brought their hearers to see something. Can't we do the same?

[2] Sources of illustrations

Every preacher I know tells me that he is poor at illustrating and that he would like to do it better. He also tells me that he would appreciate some help in sourcing illustrations. Where can he get them from?

(i) Scripture

He can get them from Scripture. When we considered exegetical accuracy we saw that the Bible is a self-interpreting book. It is also a self-illustrating book. It contains a wealth of history, biography, poetry and proverbs, all of which can be used to illustrate almost any doctrine or lesson that we teach from its pages. Seeing that even Christians know their Bibles so badly, why not always make the Bible itself your first port of call when you are looking for an illustration?

But we need to be careful. When we read the sermons of the seventeenth-century Puritans or of C. H. Spurgeon in the nineteenth century, we notice that they used every book of the Bible to illustrate what they had to say. We can't do it exactly as they did. They preached to congregations who

---

[1] Now reprinted and available from Tentmaker Publications, 121 Hartshill Road, Stoke-on-Trent ST4 7LU.

knew their Bibles well. Sometimes, then, their references to biblical events were mere allusions. They talked of shibboleths, half-shaved beards, the Valley of Baca, the potter's shop, the hem of the garment and the illness of Publius—and everyone knew what they were talking about! We can't do that today. To use these allusions as illustrations we would need to give a fuller explanation or to tell the story. In doing so, however, we would kill two birds with one stone; we would illustrate what we have to say, and we would also give our hearers a better knowledge of the whole counsel of God.

There is something else we need to be careful about. We have talked about it in an earlier chapter, but we need to say it again. We must always be careful to distinguish between the *intended* meaning of Scripture and its *illustrational* use. This distinction must also be clear to our hearers. By all means use Naaman to illustrate reluctant childlike faith, but never give the impression that this is what 2 Kings 5:1-19 is really about. By all means use the call of Samuel to illustrate the nearness of God, but do not let people imagine that the purpose of 1 Samuel chapter 3 is to get across that truth. Yes, we must certainly use other parts of Scripture to shed light on the part we are preaching from. But in doing that we do not want to obscure people's understanding of the passage we are using as an illustration!

(ii) Observation

God has given to every preacher a bank account filled, not with money, but with sermon illustrations. If we took out a thousand illustrations a day, we would never be broke. So how do we access this account? Not with a chequebook or a cash card, but with our eyes and ears. We simply keep them open, make a mental note of what we see and hear, and add a little thought.

The sights, sounds and experiences of daily life are an inexhaustible source of illustrations. Take everything you can from this shelf, and you will find that it will be re-stacked immediately. Fill up your sermon from this pump, because it never carries a 'not in use' label. Even a Duracell battery eventually runs out, but this one will never let you down. Here is a sun that always shines, a wind that always blows, a stream that never dries up, a hope that never disappoints—a supply of illustrations that never fails!

It was our Lord himself who taught us to find illustrations all around us. He talked of sowing wheat, bottling wine, building houses, leavening dough, baking loaves, borrowing from neighbours, lighting lamps, sweeping floors and finding treasures. He spoke of the duties of servants, dogs under the table, burglars breaking in, moths destroying clothes, debtors in prison, children at play, feasts, weddings, court cases and current events. He came from heaven but he lived on earth, and he spoke to the men and women of earth in pictures that they could understand. His truest followers do the same.

C. H. Spurgeon wanted all his students to be illustrative preachers. He repeatedly urged them to keep their eyes open and to reflect on what they saw. On one occasion he told them that if all they had in front of them was a candle, that single candle would provide them with enough illustrations for many sermons! They laughed. And so it was that he proved his claim by giving two addresses made up entirely of spiritual lessons that could be drawn from candles. His book, *Sermons on Candles*, is the printed version of those addresses.

Illustrations drawn from candles would not have much effect on most people today. Our is a world of electric light, television, computers, cars, mobile phones, supermarkets, designer labels, commercialised music, professional sport, world travel and hopes of exploring space. Our Lord drew his illustrations from first-century Palestine; Calvin drew his from sixteenth-century Geneva, while Spurgeon's words constantly reflect nineteenth-century London. What about us? Do our twenty-first-century hearers hear twenty-first-century illustrations? If they don't, we preachers have failed them.

(iii) Pure invention

A knowledge of the Bible, a pair of eyes, a pair of ears and a reflective mind are all that a good illustrator needs. But he can do even better if he is willing to enter the world of pure invention. Home-made parables and allegories are particularly effective. Of course, they cannot even begin to rival the parables of our Lord, but haven't *The Pilgrim's Progress* and *The Holy War* by John Bunyan proved to be a blessing to millions?

For nearly thirty years I have illustrated Paul's teaching in Romans chapter 7 by means of a simple story. It concerns a man who is walking home on a dark night. He falls into a muddy puddle, but does not realise how dirty he is until he approaches a light. He then does his best to get clean. The problem is that the nearer he gets to the light, the more he sees his filth, and the harder he tries to get clean. At last he stands right under the light and cries in despair at the sight of all the muck that is still clinging to him. 'O wretched man that I am!' (Rom. 7:24) can only be said by people close to the Lord.

Why am I mentioning this? Well, a few months ago I decided to read once more a book that I had read as a student.

I wanted to see what I thought of it now, after a gap of forty years. It is called *The Normal Christian Life* by Watchman Nee, and I was amazed to find in it the parable of the muddy puddle that I honestly thought I had invented myself! My point is this: Mr Nee's home-made parable had obviously been very effective, at least in my case, because although I was not using it as he did, it had entered so deeply into my heart that I had thought it was my own.

In my preaching I have now used home-made stories, parables and allegories many hundreds of times. On every occasion the effect has been the same; people sit up, move forward, give me the whole of their attention, and thank me afterwards. Why not reflect on what happens to your hearers on a normal day and then spin a story round it? Instead of talking abstractly about temptation, or doubt, or boldness in witnessing, why not invent scenarios which everyone will understand, and draw into them the appropriate teaching and applications? Pure invention is not deceitful. People know what you are doing. They also know that your Lord did this sort of thing two thousand years ago.

(iv) Elsewhere

In addition to the Bible and what comes to us through our senses and imagination, there are countless other sources of illustrations. As Christian preachers, we believe that all truth is God's truth. We believe that the whole world is his. We believe that we should know as little as possible about sin, and as much as possible about everything else. And so, as best we can, we make the effort to increase our knowledge in every area that is open to us—history, geography, mathematics, sciences, languages, medicine, art, literature, poetry, music, social sciences, technology, current affairs, politics, law, business, sport, communication skills, or whatever. We believe that it is right to have a hungry mind. We read books, watch television, videos and films, attend lectures, go to the theatre and concerts, take part in discussions—and ask questions wherever we go!

How much there is to know! We know only the tiniest part of it. But in that tiny part there is *plenty* that we can use to illustrate our preaching. We desire knowledge for its own sake, but as we acquire it we also increase our ability to proclaim God's truth in a more interesting way.

But, once more, we must be careful. Illustrations are a tool to help people proceed from the known to the unknown. If the illustration is taken from an area that they know nothing about, it cannot usually help them. In addition, our own hearts are deceitful. It is easy to use the pulpit as a platform on which to parade how much I know. We must resist this temptation with all the strength that the Lord gives us. If we do, it will go away (James 4:7), at least for a while.

I would, however, like to plead with you to draw more illustrations from church history, despite people's almost total ignorance of it. Once more, as long as we *tell* the story and do not simply allude to it, we can kill two birds with one stone; we can use illustrations which stir the soul, while at the same time fulfilling our biblical duty to remind people of God's mighty acts. Our hearers should know about the great heroes of the faith and what we owe to them. They should know about the trials that Christ's church has been through and how it has faced them. They should be moved by tales of courage, discernment and missionary endeavour. They should be able to see that our choice of illustrations is giving back to them their history and heritage.

And I have another plea. This one concerns the Internet. God's providence has given us a fantastic resource and we should thank him for it. Yes, like everything invented and run by humans, it is horribly polluted by sin. Yes, it is a source of strong temptation and grave danger for those who do not use it with God's glory in mind. But what an asset it is to the preacher! It can provide him with substantial help in all the areas that this book deals with. There are even websites which offer tens of thousands of sermon illustrations! My plea to you is that you should use the Internet, not sinfully, not as a means of avoiding hard work, but prayerfully and sensibly—and especially for help in this area of sermon illustration, where every one of us admits that we need to do better.

[3] The selection of illustrations

If we do everything that the previous section has suggested, we shall soon have more illustrations than we can cope with! We will want to throw away many of them and to keep only the very best. So what are the characteristics of a good illustration?

(i) Subordinate

The most important thing about an illustration is that it should be subordinate. In other words, it must succeed in drawing attention to the truth that it is illustrating. Some illustrations draw attention to themselves. Others are so stimulating that they set the mind thinking about something else completely. Yet others dominate the truth by occupying a bigger place than it does. Such illustrations as these must be given the sack. They are not doing their job.

I once took a group of schoolchildren to the Louvre in Paris so that they could see the Mona Lisa. They did not appreciate it at all! It was not the famous painting that they talked about afterwards, but all the security equipment that surrounded it. They talked of lights and sensors and alarms and security doors, but they did not mention the legendary smile. It was as if they had never seen it. That electronic gadgetry reminds me of too many of my sermon illustrations!

Illustrations have no purpose *whatever* except to shed light on the truth. Preachers who have no illustrations leave us groping in oppressive gloom. Preachers who have too many illustrations expose us to the discomfort of living in a greenhouse. All we need is enough light to see the truth clearly, but nothing more.

But what if the truth we are preaching is incapable of being illustrated? This is the case, for example, with the doctrine of the Trinity. The Three-in-One-ness of God is not *like* anything! If we tried to illustrate the Trinity we would most certainly end up in heresy. This, in fact, has already happened. Some people have likened the Trinity to H_2O, which is found as ice, water and steam. Ice is not water; water is not steam; steam is not ice—but all three are H_2O; three in one! Doesn't that help people to understand?

No, it does not. The illustration serves only to teach modalism, also known as Sabellianism, which is a heresy. Modalism teaches that there is one God who reveals himself to us in three different forms, the Father, the Son and the Holy Spirit. H_2O also reveals itself to us in three different forms. The problem is that any particular molecule of H_2O does not appear as ice, water and steam all at the same time. This is precisely what modalism believes about God—the one God, when he appears as the Father, is not at that moment also the Son and the Holy Spirit. The biblical truth is very different: the Father is the whole of God, the Son is the whole of God and the Holy Spirit is the whole of God, and yet the Father is not the Son, the Son is

105

not the Holy Spirit, and the Holy Spirit is not the Father! We can put it in simple words, but we can't understand how it can be like that. Nor can we illustrate it. And if we *can't*, we shouldn't even try.

The doctrine of the Trinity is the greatest mystery of all, and next to it is the doctrine of two distinct natures in the one Person of our Lord Jesus Christ. To teach these doctrines in our preaching we should restrict ourselves to simple statements. If we use illustrations at all, it should be to point out their errors! We can then correct them with more simple statements, and thus succeed in getting the truth across.

Illustrations are to be subordinate. If they fail this test at any point, they are to be abandoned. God has called us to proclaim his *truth*, not to pervert it or dumb it down.

(ii) Clear

Illustrations have no value if they are not clear. Some are so complicated that all they do is confuse the audience. There are preachers who spend time explaining their illustrations, and even illustrating them! But why turn the lights out when it is your job to turn them on?

I have a friend who is a faithful minister today, but who was once an inexperienced theological student who invited me to hear him preach. The content of his message was fine. Its beginning, however, was a disaster. He began by telling the congregation about the Great Pyramid, but it quickly became clear that they knew nothing about it. He therefore spent several minutes explaining where it was, when it was built, and why. He then tried to introduce his sermon by drawing a lesson from the Pyramid's construction, a subject also about which they knew nothing. The history lesson therefore continued, mixed up with lots of information about civil engineering. The whole sermon lasted about thirty-five minutes, ten of which had been spent on the Great Pyramid! Preachers, beware! Illustrations must be clear; in fact, they must be so clear that it is impossible to miss the point that they are getting across.

(iii) Brief

They must also be brief. If an illustration is drawn out and filled with a host of unimportant and irrelevant details, it will bore your congregation to distraction. Forget all the minor roads, get on the motorway and take your people from A to B as directly as possible! In the matter of illustrations it is the destination that counts, not the journey.

However, if you do embark on a long illustration, please have the courtesy to finish it. I once began to read a fascinating article in a weekend magazine. It was about the lifestyle and views of Prince Charles, and was telling me things of which I knew nothing. I got to the bottom of the page and turned over. But the article did not continue! Nor was there any further trace of it in the entire magazine. I felt frustrated and cheated.

There are preachers who behave like that. They begin an illustration but quickly realise that it is either irrelevant or too long. So they dump it and get on with their sermon. It is true that congregations do not like long illustrations, unless they happen to be stories, parables or allegories. But nor do they like to be left guessing what happened next. And why should they be thinking about that anyway? Don't you want them to give the whole of their mind to the rest of the sermon?

(iv) Dignified

Whether our illustrations are short or long, they all need to be dignified. Is it not *divine* truth that we are preaching?

Can we shed light on holy things by drawing pictures from what is coarse, indelicate or frivolous? There is no place for bad taste in the Christian life, so there is certainly no place for it in the Christian pulpit.

A close French friend once took me to see the magnificent cathedral of Le Puy. It towers above a picturesque town and seems more impressive with every step that you climb up towards it. One of its treasures is a medieval picture that hangs over the high altar. It portrays an elderly white-bearded gentleman sitting on some clouds. He is supposed to be *God*!

The pilgrims and tourists are attracted to that picture and encourage others to come and see it too. They pray in front of it and buy postcards of it afterwards. But, in fact, it degrades God. It is a blasphemy. Its very existence is a violation of his law. It robs him of his majesty and does nothing to stir up worship in any believing heart. Yes, the fact that a picture is popular does not mean that it is legitimate. The same is true of word-pictures. They must be dignified. They must reverence the truth that they are attempting to illustrate.

Does this mean that we can never use humour in the pulpit? My own view is that we should not normally plan to be funny, but if humour comes out entirely naturally it may often be a good thing, as long as it is pure. There are many traces of humour in the Bible, such as Elijah's stinging words to the prophets of Baal (1 Kings 18:27) or our Lord's parable of the friend at midnight (Luke 11:5-8). Such humour is not usually used to teach doctrine, although there are exceptions. It is mostly used to drive truth home and, in particular, to show up hypocrisy and insincerity. If we keep the principle of *subordination* in mind, we shall not make too many mistakes in this area.

(v) Varied

In addition to all that we have said so far, illustrations need to be varied. Despite C. H. Spurgeon's extraordinary ability to draw countless lessons from candles, I am glad to note that he never preached a sermon where all the illustrations were drawn from this source. If he had done so, modern analysts would have diagnosed him as suffering from compulsive obsessive disorder!

What would the countryside be like if there was only one shade of green? And what is a sermon like where all the illustrations are taken from the preacher's family life, or from his hobby, or (worst of all?) from football? We all know what 'sameness' is and we tire of it. People who work in sweet factories can eat as many sweets as they like during working hours, but before long they are not eating any at all. Variety really is the spice of life.

We are ambassadors of the God who gave the seasons and who painted all the colours of the rainbow. He filled this world with a multiplicity of species and gave to every face a different shape. Even within his own undivided being there is diversity. If we maintain variety by drawing our sermon illustrations from all the sources we mentioned earlier, we will do him an honour.

(vi) Accurate

The last thing that needs to be said is that our illustrations should be accurate. We cannot illustrate truth by being *un*truthful. We must not say things happened to us when they did not. If we refer to history, biography, or any other field of knowledge, we must get our facts right. If people find us to be an unreliable source of information about ordinary things, what will they think when we talk to them about the things of God?

I once used an illustration based on the structure of the solar system. People were interested, but several of them were making strange faces. As soon as the service was over a queue quickly formed at the door. Each person wanted to tell me the same thing: the planets were not in the order that I had said! I was embarrassed. I was also ashamed. I had preached an error as if it were a fact and had therefore strangled my own credibility. A slip of the tongue is one thing. An avoidable error is another.

Our illustrations must be accurate factually and they must also be accurate theologically. Do we need to say any more about the H_2O illustration? That is an obvious perversion of the truth. But an accurate illustration in a doctrinal area can be a very powerful tool. For example, some people have come to a better understanding of what happens at conversion simply by being told of the birth of a baby. Does the baby cry out *in order to* be born or because it *has been* born? In the same way our cry to the Lord to save us is the proof of the new birth, and not its cause.

Once more, the principle of *subordination* will guide us through all the dangers that confront us here. A theologically inaccurate illustration can never serve the truth, but an accurate one can drive it into the memory for ever.

* * *

It is time to close this chapter. I am appealing to us all to make sure that every message we preach is vividly illustrated. Our people cannot always see the shape of what we are trying to describe to them. Let's switch the lights on! We must not have so much light that we leave them dazzled and still unable to see. We must not have chandeliers that leave them gasping in amazement. Ordinary lights will do. And we will know that our sermon has done some good when we hear them say, 'Now I see what he's getting at!'

* * *

Something to do

1. You have a friend who illustrates easily and liberally, but people who listen to him say that he is just a story-teller? What are you going to say to him?

2. Illustrate three doctrines from what you can see in the room where you are sitting.

3. What illustrations would you use to help you in a sermon on Ephesians 2:8-9?

5
Pointed Application

I have never been to a tailor because I have always bought my suits off the peg. I have heard, though, that there are still a lot of people who have their clothes made to measure. It is with this thought in mind that I would like to begin this chapter.

Imagine a tailor who weaves his own cloth. There are no flaws in the threads (exegetical accuracy). It is strong, high-quality material (doctrinal substance). It is woven into an attractive pattern (clear structure). Even an ordinary person can see and feel how good it is (vivid illustration). So there is nothing to complain about, is there? And yet we all know that the tailor has not finished his work.

A tailor's job is to make clothes for people. His customers come in all shapes and sizes, and with very different needs. He must do more than make choice cloth; he must cut it to fit each customer so that they can wear it every day. A tailor who can't do this should not be in the business.

All that we do as preachers is wasted if our hearers do not wear our material every day of the week. They are to be doers of the Word, and not hearers only (James 1:22). It is a mistake to preach 'one size fits all' sermons. The people who listen to us must all wear the same material, but we must cut it so that it fits each one individually, and so that they can wear it with ease in their particular circumstances. Off-the-peg ministry will not do. If God's truth is going to be worn honourably in this world, sermons must be *tailor-made*.

[1] What pointed application is

(i) Definition

John A. Broadus preached with power in the southern states of nineteenth-century America. His book, *The Preparation and Delivery of Sermons*, is a classic. Although the book is not too easy to read, every page is filled with clear teaching and sound advice. Why not take a few minutes to reflect on every word of his definition of application? It goes like this:

> Application, in the strict sense, is that part, or those parts, of the discourse in which we show how the subject applies to the persons addressed, what practical instructions it offers them, what practical demands it makes upon them.[1]

Daniel Webster, the American thinker and educator, also lived and wrote in the nineteenth century. On one occasion he famously said, 'When a man preaches to me, I want him to make it a personal matter, a personal matter, a personal matter.'[2]

Like the rays of the sun focused on the skin by a magnifying glass, application focuses the burning claims of truth on the conscience of the hearer. It preaches *to* the people and not just *in front of* them. It isolates each individual and makes him understand that the message is for

---

[1] Broadus, John A., *On the Preparation and Delivery of Sermons* (London, Hodder & Stoughton, undated), p. 211.
[2] Quoted by John A. Broadus, p. 210.

him personally. It confronts him. It comes to him like a court official knocking at the door of his heart and handing him a personal summons. It demands a response and insists that it should be given there and then.

(ii) Importance

Where there is no application, preaching has no soul, no life and no interest. It carries no striking conviction to the conscience and no healing comfort to the heart. It leaves each hearer feeling like a child who has never been hugged and who has never been smacked. Poor child! Whatever will become of him? He will go through life bewildered and disturbed, without moorings and without values.

Preaching without application is like shooting an arrow into the air in the hope that it may perhaps strike someone, somewhere. In the providence of God it may do just that, as King Ahab unhappily discovered in 1 Kings 22:34-35. Aimless sermons do sometimes accomplish something! God's normal way of working, however, is quite different. When the Welsh archers at the Battle of Agincourt shot into the air, they knew exactly what they were doing. Their aim proved true and they destroyed the French.

A surgeon's calling is to heal, and the instrument he uses is a knife. Without his knife he cannot heal, but if he does not know where to cut he will kill the patient. The preacher must be even more careful. Application may save a soul, while the failure to apply may ruin it for ever. Application that is suitable for one person may damage another beyond recovery.

Where there is no pointed application there is no true preaching. We have a lot to learn from the apostles. Their letters are filled with doctrine, but the writers do not then say, 'Well, there it is, I have explained the doctrine; I will now leave it to the Holy Spirit to show you how these truths should be worked out in practice.' No! No! and no! They spell it out in black and white. They plead with their readers to lead a life worthy of the calling with which they have been called (Eph. 4:1). They show them in detail what this means, talking to them about their individual lives, and their behaviour in the church, in the family and in society. They deal with specific sins, specific duties, specific problems, specific opportunities and specific joys, and in this way give us a model to follow.

The pointed application which is part and parcel of true biblical preaching has no parallel in the unconverted world. Speech-making was a very important part of life in ancient Greece and Rome, but application in public was not encouraged. You won't find it in Plato or Aristotle, or in their followers. But you will find it in Paul, Chrysostom, Wickliffe, Luther, Calvin, Owen, Bunyan, Whitefield, Wesley, Spurgeon, Lloyd-Jones and Hugh Morgan! You cannot explain the power of the Christian pulpit without considering the question of application. When Christ sends a man to preach, he commissions him not only to tell the truth, but also to tell his hearers how it works out in practice.

But unconverted men and women don't like to hear application. Nor do unspiritual believers. I remember once preaching at a Bible convention in the Jura Mountains that divide France from Switzerland. A large number of Christians had gathered from both countries. One of them was a pastor who became increasingly agitated while I was preaching. Immediately after the meeting he said to me angrily, 'Monsieur Olyott, my people are not children, and they are not fools either. When you preach the Word they are perfectly capable of working out for themselves how it should be put into practice. They don't need you to spell it out so directly!'

I admit that my preaching is far from perfect, but that man was wrong. The human heart is wicked and it does not want to change. It is very happy for the Word to be preached as long as it is not pressed upon the conscience. It can see how God's truth applies to others but does not want to accept it for itself. It acts with selfish unselfishness and passes the buck. Preaching will not get anywhere if it is not applied to the people in front of us. We must press it on them and chase them with it, because if we don't they will think that it is saying nothing to them personally. But how is this to be done?

[2] How pointed application is to be made

(i) Be specific

We are preachers. Preaching is about change, and that is *all* that it is about. We have not been called to speak in a vague and general way, or merely to explain principles, but to speak about sin, to point to Christ, and to talk to people bluntly about the duties and comforts of the gospel. Writing for another generation, Charles Bridges put it like this: 'Preaching, in order to be effective, must be reduced from vague generalities, to a tangible individual character —coming home to every man's business, and even to his bosom.'[3]

Look at how our Lord did it in Matthew 19:21. He could see that the rich young ruler had an idol, not in his home but in his heart. He was a religious materialist who loved his money more than he loved his Maker. Our Lord did not

---

[3] Bridges, Charles, *The Christian Ministry* (London, The Banner of Truth Trust, 1958), p. 271.

give him a lecture on the principles underlying idolatry and then leave him to think through what he might have to do as a result. He told him to go home, smash his idol, think of the eternal reward and follow his Lord: 'If you want to be perfect, go, sell what you have and give to the poor, and you will have treasure in heaven; and come, follow me.'

Look at what our Lord did in John 4:15-16. He had brought the immoral Samaritan woman to the point where she showed some personal interest in the living water he was talking about. His next move was not to tell her, in some general way, that she should repent of her past life. He made her face it. 'Go, call your husband, and come here', he said. And we know what followed.

Look at what our Lord did in Mark 7:20-23. He was dealing with people who did not understand about heart pollution, so he showed them their error and taught them a general principle: 'What comes out of a man, that defiles a man.' That is where many modern preachers would stop. They would say no more, but would leave people to think through what this actually means. Our Lord was not like that at all. He spelled it all out in the most black-and-white way that anyone can imagine:

> For from within, out of the heart of men, proceed evil thoughts, adulteries, fornications, murders, thefts, covetousness, wickedness, deceit, licentiousness, an evil eye, blasphemy, pride, foolishness. All these evil things come from within and defile a man.

Look at how the apostle Paul followed so closely his Lord's method. In Galatians 5:16-18 he told his readers that in this world there are two sorts of behaviour. One sort is inspired by the Spirit and the other by 'the lust of the flesh'. If you go the Spirit's way you won't go the other way, even though you might find it appealing. Rules won't keep you from going the wrong way, but going the Spirit's way will!

What Paul wrote is clear, but it raises a question; did the Galatians *really* know which way was which? Paul was a preacher, and he did not leave them in any doubt:

> Now the works of the flesh are evident, which are: adultery, fornication, uncleanness, licentiousness, idolatry, sorcery, hatred, contentions, jealousies, outbursts of wrath, selfish ambitions, dissensions, heresies, envy, murders, drunkenness, revels, and the like; of which I tell you beforehand, just as I also told you in time past, that those who practise such things will not inherit the kingdom of God. But the fruit of the Spirit is love, joy, peace, long-suffering, kindness, goodness, faithfulness, gentleness, self-control. Against such there is no law.
>
> (Gal. 5:19-23)

After such a paragraph every Galatian reader would have known in detail the difference between a non-Christian and a Christian character. In the same way the apostle spelled out to Timothy that there are two sorts of people on earth, the righteous and the lawless. But what, concretely, does lawlessness look like? Once more, the apostle followed his Lord's method of teaching:

> The law is not made for a righteous person, but for the lawless and insubordinate, for the ungodly and for sinners, for the unholy and profane, for killers of fathers and killers of mothers, for murderers, for fornicators, for male homosexuals, for kidnappers, for liars, for perjurers, and if there is any other thing that is contrary to sound doctrine, according to the glorious gospel of the blessed God which was committed to my trust.
>
> (1 Tim. 1:9-11)

Neither our Lord nor his apostle was satisfied with general statements. They put flesh on them. They gave lists of examples of what they were talking about. If application is too general it ceases to be application. The preacher's target is always the conscience. He reaches the conscience via the mind, and expects the conscience to motivate the life. He storms it, he asks it questions, and he insists that it should reflect and act in the light of the truth preached.

John Jones of Talsarn, one of the greatest preachers of nineteenth-century Wales, sometimes commented on his method of preaching. He said that he always went into the pulpit carrying several bombs. He would throw one into the congregation fairly early in the sermon and watch it kill a few people. He would keep throwing bombs throughout the sermon until every one of his hearers was 'slain'!

What did he mean? John Jones believed in application and kept on applying the Word in different ways until he could see that it had had an effect on every person present. The most powerful preachers in history have always done the same. A sermon in print is nothing like the real thing, but we can see this feature in the preaching of such men as John Wesley, George Whitefield and Jonathan Edwards. The Puritans had done it before them, always accompanying their exposition and doctrine with what they called 'uses'. These 'uses', or applications, were often very numerous, and their chief characteristic was that they spoke very *specifically* to their congregations about their sins, duties, problems and privileges. Does our failure to speak as specifically as they did partly explain our lack of power in preaching today?

(ii) Be discriminating
When we stand up to preach and look across the congregation, we can be sure that there will be many different sorts

of people present. Perhaps there is a visitor who has had little or no previous contact with the gospel. There is probably someone who attends church regularly but who does not appear to be converted. There is a person who has 'made a decision for Christ' who does not yet show any sign of being truly alive spiritually. There are others who are not yet saved but who are seeking the Lord earnestly. There are new converts. There are mature saints. There are believers who are going through strong temptation, doubt, or trouble. There are those who have become increasingly self-centred and whose spiritual walk has become tired and jaded. There are children who are happy to be there and others who just put up with it. There is a bored teenager with his head in his hands. And so we could go on. Who knows how many different sorts of people we could put on the list?

What are we going to do with all these people? Are we going to put the medicine on the counter and say, 'Here you are, folks! It will do you good. Just take the dosage that you think will suit you!'? Or, like a responsible pharmacist, are we going to give to them what is right for each one *individually*?

In public preaching, of course, we do not focus on individuals or name anybody. But when a truth preached, each group of people needs to know how that truth applies to them, and each individual present needs to be able to say to himself, 'There was something in that message for *me*.'

Let us go to immoral first-century Corinth and let us spend a moment with the Christian church there. A letter has arrived from the apostle Paul! Everyone sits still as someone reads it out. At a certain moment there is a particular hush:

Do you not know that the unrighteous will not inherit the kingdom of God? Do not be deceived. Neither fornicators, nor idolaters, nor adulterers, nor homosexuals, nor sodomites, nor thieves, nor covetous, nor drunkards, nor revilers, nor extortioners will inherit the kingdom of God. And such were some of you. But you were washed, but you were sanctified, but you were justified in the name of the Lord Jesus and by the Spirit of our God.

(1 Cor. 6:9-11)

Can you imagine how each person felt as their particular sin was read out? Can you imagine the sense of relief that spread over the congregation as the last two sentences were read? Would there have been such a deep sense of relief and wonder if the apostle had simply written, 'Some of your sins have been terrible, but God has forgiven them all'? There is power in application which is not only specific, but which speaks to definite groups of people.

There is a book in English that God has used to bring spiritual life to tens of thousands of people. It was written by the Puritan Joseph Alleine and it is called *An Alarm to the Unconverted*. Alleine mentions ten sorts of people who are openly and obviously unconverted. He then refers to twelve secret marks of being unconverted. In other words, he shows that there are twenty-two sorts of unconverted people and he addresses each sort in turn without butchering any single verse of the Bible.[4] If God has described unconverted men and women so differently, should not we also detect that these types exist, and speak to them accordingly?

What does all this mean in practice? Before I stand up to preach, I should reflect on who I am going to preach to.

---

[4] See chapter 4, 'The Marks of the Unconverted' in Alleine, Joseph, *An Alarm to the Unconverted* (London, The Banner of Truth Trust, 1959), pp. 44-53.

I should think about the congregation I will have, and not the congregation I would *like* to have! What does my passage have to say to that young lad at junior school? How is it to be applied to that teenager, and to that student who is back with her parents for the vacation? In what particular ways does it speak to the young married couples, the would-be missionary, that single person in her forties, the unemployed, the widow, the sad, the lonely, the elderly, the ill and the disturbed?

It is not enough to prepare top-quality cloth. The time has come to cut it. Every person present must see that you have hung in the pulpit a set of clothes which will fit them exactly. But that is not all; you must urge them to put them on. This brings us to our final point.

(iii) Be persuasive

Our hearers need to know not only that the clothes *should* be worn, but also that they *can* be worn, and that it is definitely in their interest to do so. The preacher has not done his job if he only tells people *what* to do; he must also tell them *how* to do it and *why* it is worth doing. The Bible is always clear on the *what*. The *why* is covered by its general teaching on the blessings of obedience—blessings that we enjoy both in this life and the next. The *how* is covered by its teaching on wisdom, and here the preacher may need to make some wise practical suggestions which would benefit his people, rather than speaking with the direct authority of the Word. But it is not an area that he can neglect. He would not be loving his hearers if he did that.

Scolding is not usually the best way of persuading people to do something worthwhile. God's Word has quite a lot to say about nagging women and none of it is positive! Faithful preachers are blunt about sin and equally blunt about the need of repentance, but, as men who care for people, they still prefer the carrot to the stick. Parents who love their children chastise them when necessary, but spend a lot more of their time giving them encouragement and treats. A puppy learns obedience more quickly through rewards of chocolate drops than through stern words and beatings.

As a young preacher I was once invited to speak at some special meetings in a small town in South Wales. I found the chapel more quickly than I expected and so arrived before it opened. Two elderly ladies were already waiting outside. 'Are you coming to the meetings?' I asked. 'Yes,' they said, 'We are coming to hear the Whip!'

The Whip? The ladies, who had evidently not recognised me, told me that they had heard the guest preacher some months before. What a whipping he had given them! They weren't sure how they would get on with him today, but they were giving him the benefit of the doubt and were coming to hear him again.

I don't need to tell you that they were embarrassed when they suddenly realised that it was 'the Whip' they were speaking to! But they weren't as embarrassed as I was to have been given such a nickname. I learned a great deal from those two saints. They did nothing to lessen my desire to be direct and frank, but they showed me that ticking people off and persuading them are two different things.

Persuasion sets out to show people that the suit you have tailored is worth wearing. It tells them of the happiness and blessedness that will come into their life if they put God's truth into practice. It explains what dangers they will avoid, what spiritual progress they will make, what experiences they may have and how obedience pleases their Redeemer. It leaves people not just willing but *wanting* to walk God's way.

Over the years I have spent a lot of time taking young people walking over the hills and mountains of North Wales. They always moan about how much kit I make them carry! Why can't they just take a few sandwiches and a drink? Why do I insist on certain spare clothes, a hat, waterproof jackets and leggings, a first-aid kit, a whistle, a torch, emergency rations, a litre of water, a bivvy bag and a number of other items—and all that on a summer day? I then explain to them what has happened to other walkers and why each item is needed. The moaning ceases, the rucksacks are picked up, and we enjoy the day! Saying, 'Just bring what I tell you, or you can't come', would not have the same effect.

Persuasion is part of life, but all too frequently it is not part of preaching. How many boys do you know who like football but who don't like the twice-weekly training sessions? Then they learn that if they are fitter than the other team, can run faster and for longer, and can dance around them through developed skill, they can win almost every time! The thought of regular wins makes athletes out of couch potatoes. A kilo of persuasion is worth a tonne of rebukes.

But real persuasion involves passion. I shall have a little more to say about this in a later chapter, but something must be said now. Some preachers do not like any display of emotion, and some teachers of preachers actively discourage it. They need to remember that you can't persuade anyone of anything unless your soul is in it. Persuasive speech is filled with feeling. Persuasive preachers speak of evil with disgust, of Christ with warmth, of Christians with love, and of heaven with excitement! They are stirred in the very depths of their being, and every adult and child in front of them is aware of it. Preachers standing like statues who intone without feeling do nothing to persuade people. They have lost the human touch. Why listen to an expressionless giver of facts when you can find the same information in colour on the Internet?

Let's go back to the Great War of 1914–18. A group of frightened soldiers are standing behind sandbags in a muddy trench. In a few minutes a whistle will blow and they will have to scamper up ladders, leap over the sandbags and run through a hail of gunfire towards the enemy. Many will die at once, others will bleed to death in no man's land, and only a few will return. How do you motivate men like that? How do you persuade them to get up those ladders and to race towards almost certain destruction?

The sergeant speaks to them with deep feeling in his voice. He explains to them what is at stake in this war. If it is lost, freedom will be lost. Their parents will be slaughtered, their wives may be raped and their children will be enslaved. Everything they have ever valued will be gone for ever. This battle is important. In fact, it is vitally important. If it is won, the war will not be won, but at least victory will be one step nearer. At this point the sergeant checks his weapon, blows his whistle, and cries with a conquering passion, 'Come on! Forward!'

Where there is no passion there is no persuasion. If the general himself had come and given the same facts, but had done it in icy tones without a touch of feeling, force or intensity, the battle would have been lost. The men would have been discouraged and filled with doubts. Duty would have taken them up the ladders, but not to victory.

However true they may be, the only words that reach the heart are those that come from the heart. Preachers will never stir anyone unless they are stirred themselves.

* * *

The final test of a sermon, however, is not what people feel while it is being preached. We have just seen that the 'thrill' of the moment is important, and that the sermon cannot accomplish its purpose without it. Nonetheless, the big question is still this one: has the truth *preached* become a truth *practised*?

One Monday morning our imaginary tailor walked round the small town where he had preached to twenty people each Sunday for the last few months. He knew them quite well now and decided to bump into each one of them if he could. He saw James and Mary waiting for the bus that would take them to school. He chatted with Monica who worked in the bank. He had a coffee with Stephen who was not going back to university until next week. He dropped by the supermarket, the clinic, the petrol station, the library, the solicitors, the flower shop, the town hall and even the tax office. At last he had ticked off nineteen names, so he returned home to have lunch with the twentieth, his wife. He noticed that she too, like all the rest, was wearing the tailor-made clothes he had prepared. So he went upstairs to wash his hands before eating, crept into the bedroom, knelt down and thanked God.

* * *

Something to do

1. You are going to preach in a church that you have never visited before and where you know no one at all. What can you do to make sure that your sermon is filled with meaningful application?

2. Your new minister is so concerned about preaching pointedly that he has become censorious. Give him some advice.

3. Outline a sermon on Ezekiel 37:1-14 and list your applications.

6
Helpful Delivery

When is a book *not* a book? It is easy for me to answer this question. I am sitting in front of a computer into which I have typed everything you have read so far. It's going to be a book but it isn't one yet. A book has no existence until it has been printed and bound.

When is a sermon *not* a sermon? When the exegesis has been completed, the doctrine gathered, the structure put together, the illustrations sifted, the applications prepared and the final version of the notes written up, there is still no sermon—no sermon at all! A sermon has no existence until it has been preached.

This is why the delivery of the sermon is of crucial importance. The best-prepared message in the world will be of little value if it is delivered poorly. The hard work of hours and days can be lost in a moment. A baby can be conceived in the womb and can grow perfectly until the moment of its birth, and then break its parents' hearts by coming into the world lifeless.

As I think I have told you before, I have come to a stage in my life where I hear a lot of sermons. Because of the circles I move in, I have very few grumbles about their content. But almost all of them are put across badly. This is because preachers are not giving as much attention to the delivery of their sermons as they are to their preparation. They are going into the pulpit with a sense of closure. They are saying to themselves, 'I have a sermon', not realising that the only sermon that ever exists is the one that people take away with them. They are careful in the way they get their sermons ready, and yet they are negligent, even shoddy, in the way they communicate them.

This will not do. Poorly delivered sermons do not glorify God. They disappoint his people, slow down the spread of the gospel and provoke a great deal of scorn. Every preacher needs to evaluate his delivery every time he speaks. He will not improve automatically. He may even get worse, especially if his bad habits become so ingrained that he cannot shake them off. If we neglect the subject of delivery, it may soon be too late. May I ask you, then, to consider the following seven aspects?[1]

[1] Your spirit

The preaching that you do cannot be divorced from the *you* that does it! As you speak to men and women, something of your *spirit* comes across to them, and it cannot be hidden. The most famous statement of this unbreakable link between the preacher and his preaching is that found in Phillips Brooks' lecture on 'The Two Elements of Preaching' in his 1877 Lyman Beecher lectures:

Preaching is the communication of truth by man to men. It has in it two essential elements, truth and personality. Neither of those can it spare and still be preaching . . . Preaching is the bringing of truth through personality . . .

---

[1] I first had my attention drawn to these seven points by reading Gibbs, Alfred P., *Preach the Word* (Oak Park, Illinois, Emmaus, 1958). What follows is based on his outline, although amended and altered quite considerably. I want however to record how profoundly thankful I am for that book and to record how much it helped me through my first stumbling attempts to preach.

The truth is in itself a fixed and stable element; the personality is a varying and growing element.[2]

We all have different characters and personalities. There are, however, some qualities that must be true of every preacher. First of all, we must be *courageous*. We are called to stand in the line of those who have been true to God whatever may have been the opinions of men and women—the line in which stand Moses, Elijah, Jeremiah, John the Baptist, our Lord Jesus Christ, the apostles, the martyrs, the Reformers like Martin Luther and John Knox, the revivalists of the eighteenth century, and countless others. We are bearers of the Word of God! We preach the despised cross. Our message is filled with comfort, but we have no sugary words for the unrepentant and no thoughts of compromise with the ungodly spirit of the times.

We must be *humble*. We know that pride, our chief occupational hazard, can ruin our ministries and rob us of our power. We are certainly not going to be apologetic for the message that we bring: 'If anyone speaks, let him speak as the oracles of God' (1 Pet. 4:11). However, we cannot be faithful to the gospel of the self-humiliating Christ if we preach it with a self-important air. We will fall into pride every day if we forget our sin, our Saviour's cross, and the fact that we cannot accomplish anything at all without his blessing.

We must be *sincere*. People, and young people in particular, hate sham. It is sad to say that they half expect it in a preacher. We must be truthful enough to avoid giving the impression that we are perfect, and holy enough for all to

---

[2] Phillips Brooks, *Lectures on Preaching*, the 1877 Yale Lectures (Grand Rapids, Baker, 1969), pp. 5, 28.

know that we practise what we preach. We can undo our whole ministry by living inconsistently. We all know that those who are sincere exercise a fascinating power over us that is hard to put into words. The only way to speak like a sincere person is to *be* one!

We must be *earnest*. We are back to the whole question of feeling, which is so little emphasised today. We must believe what we say, we must mean what we say, and we must *feel* what we say. Do we care about the people in front of us, or don't we? Their eternal destiny depends on their reaction to what we are saying; how can we be unmoved? It is inexcusable to have a sleepy delivery when eternal issues are at stake, but such a delivery cannot be manufactured. We must feel the sheer force of truth in the depths of our souls; then we will speak persuasively enough.

We must be *self-possessed*. If we know our material well, believe it in our hearts and prepare our sermon thoroughly, our delivery will be confident and composed. Sincerity and earnestness will then move us to express it persuasively. Where there is no self-possession, preachers come across as raving fanatics. Where there is no self-abandonment, they come across as unfeeling statues. There must be both fuel and fire. A fire without fuel quickly goes out, while fuel without fire is cold and miserable. We really must have both and we must be satisfied with nothing less! I am glad to know that a disciple who *spends time* with the Risen Lord, listening to his voice in the Scriptures, will be led into an Emmaus Road experience where his heart will *burn* within him (Luke 24:32).

We must be *courteous*. Nobody must preach unless they know the difference between being forthright and being rude. If we offend people, it must *never* be by the way we say things, but *only* by what God's Word contains. Coarse illustrations, bad manners, vulgar words and a hostile manner have no place in the Christian pulpit. Nor must the preacher scold those who are present for the sins of those who are absent!

We must be *good-humoured*. There is 'a time to weep and a time to laugh' (Eccl. 3:4). We have already said a little about humour in the pulpit, but let us now say a little more. It is fatal to mix up being serious with being sombre. Of course, there are some things that should never be laughed about, such as God, the atonement, death, judgement, heaven and hell. But when humour can be the servant of truth (and, surely, this is the great principle), let us not be afraid to use it. It can relieve emotional pressure, help concentration, capture those who are hostile to us, assault hypocrisy, show how ridiculous some ideas are, and prove to our hearers that we are human. If God has put such a tool in our hands, can it be right to throw it away?

[2] Your language

How do we get our message across to the people in front of us? By words! If those words are clear and forceful, the message will be clear and forceful. Words are the vehicle by which what is in our mind gets into theirs. All the other factors mentioned in this chapter may help or hinder the message, but the message itself is in *words*.

How few preachers there are who give any sustained thought to the words that they use! This is not just a major fault in those who are young and inexperienced, but also in those who have been at it for decades.

Have you ever reflected on how much the Word of God has to say about words? You might find that a few hours with a Bible and a concordance would be a real eye-opener to you. Although I have done such a study, I do not have room here to tell you all about it. All I can say to you is that the Bible teaches that our choice of words is a very important matter *indeed*. Besides, hasn't the Bible itself been given to us in the form of Spirit-chosen words?

Let's think about preaching, both past and present. Haven't many otherwise fine messages been ridiculed because of the poorly chosen, ungrammatical, badly pronounced words that the preacher has used? Haven't thousands and thousands of otherwise excellent messages provoked no response whatever, simply because they used words that people did not find easy to understand?

There can be no good delivery without the careful use of words. So what should our language be like? Here are four points that we should always remember:

Simple
Spoken English is simple when:
- We make one point per sentence.
- Most of our sentences are about ten words long.
- 90 per cent of our words are of one or two syllables.
- We do not use *any* words that our hearers do not understand *easily*.

Sentences are like building blocks; we build our sermon into people's minds one thought at a time. I have spent a good deal of my life trying to get across to preachers that an *oral style* is not the same as a *written style*, and here I am saying it again. We need to have deep thoughts, but we also need to express them simply. If the children can't understand, we are being too complicated; so we have to keep them in mind the whole time.

In a different context, the apostle Paul wrote: 'Unless you utter by the tongue words easy to understand, how will it be known what is spoken? For you will be speaking into the air' (1 Cor. 14:9). It was of our Lord that it was said: 'The common people heard him gladly' (Mark 12:37).

Grammatical

Why draw attention from the *message* to the *messenger*? This is what happens when we use incorrect English. We should not be so fussy that we end up speaking in a way that is stuffy and unnatural. The really important thing is to be *clear*, not correct. But we are not being clear if we are making mistakes that jar in people's ears.

It is not hard to speak good English. If we read lots of well-written books, we will absorb it without thinking about it. In addition, it is useful to read a few simple books on English grammar, restricting ourselves each time to a page or two, in order to let things sink in. And why not ask a good friend to note down your errors and tell you about them? It is far better that you should suffer his criticisms than that your congregation should be distracted by your use of language.

Forceful

We must choose the precise words that will *exactly* express what we want to say. If we don't, then what we *want* people to understand and what they actually *do* understand will not be the same thing.

Language cannot be forceful where the speaker uses non-words. The most popular non-words in use today are 'er' and 'um'. Young people are especially fond of using them and place them not only within their sentences, but often at the beginning as well. There is no need for them. They make the speaker sound hesitant, uncertain and stupid. They rob him of his authority. However, if you are guilty of such an irritating habit, do not try to do anything about it. Simply *notice* when you are using non-words and they will disappear on their own.

Almost as bad as non-words are what we call 'Witter words'. These are real words that add nothing to the meaning of the sentence, but whose effect is to make it sound unimportant. If you take your calling seriously, you will abandon Witter words for ever. Regular ones are 'you know?' and 'you know what I mean?' The worst is 'just'— 'Let's just pray', 'I just want to read a few verses from Mark', 'I just want to tell you'—because it gives the impression that you are almost apologising for what you are saying. All the 'just' sentences become bolder and stronger if this silly word is left out.

Correctly pronounced

Again, why distract the congregation from the message? *Nothing* must get in its way. We must all use our dictionary to learn how to pronounce any word that we are unsure of. We should also own an edition of the Authorised (King James) Version where the pronunciation of each proper name is given in the text (i.e. a pronouncing Bible). The Bible has been in English a long time now. There is a standard English way of pronouncing the name of every Bible person and place, so why stumblingly invent your own?

As far as other words are concerned, we should *never* use a word that we don't know *for certain* how to pronounce. Work on your language! Don't cause the gospel to be ridiculed because of the way that you speak when preaching it. The words you use in preaching it are its clothes—why should it be dressed in rags?

[3] Your voice

Young preachers often ask for a few simple rules to help them develop an interesting voice and to protect it from strain. I have never felt able to give them any such rules, but have preferred to pass on a few hints. The most important of these is to understand that 'the perfection of preaching is to *talk* it' (C. H. Spurgeon). In normal conversation we do not think too much about our voice. Our mind is taken up with what we want to say and what we want to happen next. If the same happens to us in preaching, we will speak well enough. Our delivery will be flowing, easy and almost conversational—I say 'almost' because it will not be *exactly* like conversation. How can it be, seeing that we will be speaking from a platform or pulpit, and not from an armchair?

Our voice will improve simply by understanding how vocal sounds are made. The voice is a wind instrument. Air in our lungs, which we push up with our diaphragm, passes over our vocal folds and causes them to vibrate. These vocal folds are in the larynx, at the top of our windpipe. The vibrations become sound waves, which are amplified by the empty spaces in our larynx, sinuses and mouth. The palate, jaws, teeth, lips and tongue change the shape of these resonating cavities and thus produce different sounds. So, to speak audibly, clearly and comfortably, we have got to learn to control our breath, not to strain the vocal folds, to exploit our resonators, and to move what changes the sound. Merely *understanding* this usually leads to some noticeable improvement.

To make our voice more interesting to listen to, we should also have an understanding of the five things that our Creator has made it able to do:

1. Pitch: it can go high or low.

2. Pace: it can go fast or slow.

3. Volume: it can be loud or soft.

4. Tone: it can, for example, be harsh or tender.

5. Emphasis: it can stress particular words in a sentence.

Remember, also, the wonderful power of the pause. What did Rudyard Kipling mean when he said, 'By your silence you shall speak'? Why did the great public speaker Cicero declare, 'The secret of rhetoric is . . . the pause'? The fact is that such thoughtful silences *always* raise attention, and can be used to bring special emphasis to words and ideas. Have you ever listened to a preacher pouring out an endless stream of words? How did you feel while it was happening? Most people find such speech to be both tiring and irritating. They switch off. They simply can't take things in if they come in an unbroken flow, with no relief. But remember: 'The pause should be long enough to call attention to the thought but not so long that the silence calls attention to the pause.'[3]

[4] Your non-verbal communication

In recent years there has been a lot of research into non-verbal communication. All the time (and we are not conscious of it!) we are broadcasting messages by means of the way we sit or stand, by our facial expressions and gestures, and by the amount of space we like around us.

[3] Robinson, Haddon W., *Expository Preaching, Principles and Practice* (Leicester, Inter-Varsity Press, 1986), p. 207. A new and updated edition of this excellent book is now available.

Because of the variety of our cultures, these signals mean different things in different places.

We dare not ignore this phenomenon! Don't ridicule it; vocal tone, smiles, frowns, stares, winks and glances *do* pass on messages, as the Word of God recognises (Prov. 6:12-14). Preaching is not just something heard; it is also something *seen*. When people watch you preach, your eyes, hands, face and feet are saying something to them. This can act for you or against you.

This must not make us unduly self-conscious. The point for us all to grasp is that our non-verbal messages must not contradict our verbal ones. What would you say about a preacher who waved two fists at the people while preaching on 'Come to me, all you who labour and are heavy laden, and I will give you rest' (Matt. 11:28)? What would you think of a man who preached on hell with both his hands in his pockets? What would you say to one who spoke on 'Silver and gold I do not have' (Acts 3:6) while he constantly played with his wedding ring? We have got to be aware of this issue. If we are, our unhelpful signals will largely cure themselves.

Hand-in-hand with what we are considering goes the question of *eye contact*—an area where even many experienced preachers fail dismally. Look at your people! *Look* at them! Look the whole world in the face while you preach!

You have no more useful means of non-verbal communication than this one. Eye contact commands attention—who will concentrate on a message given by a person who never looks at anybody? Look them in the eyes, and each one will feel that the message is for them *personally*. Yes, during the message, connect with every single person in the place *while you are actually talking*. Don't treat them as a crowd, but as the individuals that they are.

Where a preacher has good eye contact, people are likely to take him seriously. We all distrust people who won't look us in the eyes. We think of them as untrustworthy and shifty, as people who are trying to hide something from us. No gospel preacher should be giving out such a message, however unintentionally. So let your people see your face; let them see that you are looking at them.

Besides, eye contact has another advantage. It enables you to see how people are reacting to your message. Do they look interested? Confused? Bored? Excited? Troubled? Hostile? Pleased? Are they beginning to get weary? Is it time for an illustration to arrest their attention? If you don't *look* at your congregation, you can't answer any of these questions.

All preachers who love their people are keen on eye contact. How else would they spot the troubled person to whom they may be able to say a helpful personal word afterwards? How else can they see whether their congregation is comfortable or not—too hot, too cold, dazzled by the sun, trying to cope with insufficient light, or whatever? Normally these things will not be put right unless the man at the front takes action—and, Mr Preacher, that man at the front is *you*!

This is not a time to look over their heads, to stare down at your notes, to gaze out of the windows or to shut your eyes, but to look people in the eyes and to unashamedly give them the Word of God.

[5] Your appearance

In thinking about sermon delivery we must also give our attention to our personal appearance and to our clothes. We may be tempted to think that this subject is of little or no importance, but we would be wrong. This is because the way I appear makes a difference to the way my hearers respond to me. The subject, then, is of burning interest.

However, we must be careful to avoid laying down hard and fast rules in this area. There aren't any. Fashions in grooming and styles of clothing are constantly changing. This said, every preacher in the world must remember the following principle: *nothing must draw people's attention away from the message to the messenger; nor must anything be allowed to dishonour or shame the message.*

As someone who preaches the Word in twenty-first-century Britain, I would regard the following as essential in my situation:

- Neat combed hair.
- No excess weight.
- Deodorised body, clean teeth and sweet breath.
- Dress as a man who has something important to say. In my culture that is a suit, shirt and tie. This is how our representatives dress in Parliament. It is also the dress of consultant doctors, successful salesmen—and most well-known football managers!
- Clean shoes, trousers pressed, no bulging pockets, clean shirt and well-tied tie.

Again and again I have found myself distracted from the Word by the dress of the men who proclaimed it. It is not pleasant spending an hour or more gazing at a massive coffee stain twelve inches under a man's chin, a laughing skier on a bright red pullover, or two well-known cartoon characters printed on the preacher's T-shirt! More than once, very ill people have told me that they could not take their visiting ministers seriously, because although they had read the Scriptures and prayed, they had come dressed in football shirts. We will not all agree on what is and what is not permissible, but we must all agree that this is an area that we need to think about more deeply.

[6] Your movement and gestures

It is important that we keep calling to mind that preaching is something that is *seen* as well as heard. Before we preachers learn to move in the pulpit we should first of all learn to *stand*. We should stand as heralds, uprightly but not stiffly. This means having our weight evenly distributed on both our feet throughout the whole message. It means not clinging on to the preaching desk, but learning simply to stand with our arms hanging down when they are not being used. This seems awkward at first, but you soon get used to it and, of course, it makes breathing easier. It means *never* putting any hand in any pocket, in case we give the impression of being casual. It means a lifelong ban on scratching, fidgeting, twiddling our fingers or fiddling with our ears, hair or glasses. It means sometimes leaning on the lectern to make a friendly or intimate point, but returning to the normal stance afterwards.

What do we do with our bodies, heads and hands during normal conversation, especially if we are standing? We do not normally use them to work off nervous energy, but to help us get across what we are saying, and, if necessary, to describe it more fully. We should do exactly the same in preaching. If we remember that preaching should be like conversation done in public, we will avoid most of the major mistakes.

We must not be afraid to be seen and we must not be afraid to move! If we have any choice in the matter, we should speak from positions where people can see us from head to toe. We have hidden behind wooden fences for far too long and it has not helped us to communicate. A man with a message speaks with his whole body, and not just his head and shoulders. The time has come to give the traditional pulpit an honourable burial, and for us to speak from platforms where we can be easily seen.

Whether we use pulpit or platform, our gestures can either help people to understand or hinder them. When properly used, gestures help us make our point more forcibly. Our hearers are driven to look at us, to keep looking at us, and to give us their entire attention. They see what we are driving at and enter into it more completely. And something happens to us as well; we feel increasingly at ease.

What are the characteristics of helpful gestures? Haddon W. Robinson tells us that they are:[4]

- *Spontaneous*, not planned. They come out naturally because of our feeling about what we are saying.

- *Definite*, not half-hearted or awkward. We put our body into them.

- *Varied*, because any repeated gesture soon becomes irritating and distracts from the message.

- *Properly timed*, preceding or accompanying the point that is being made. If they follow it, they look ridiculous.

In church history there are many stories of preachers practising their gestures in front of mirrors! Personally I do not think that this is a good idea. I am sure it must make the preacher quite self-conscious about what he is doing, and thus break the first of Robinson's rules. However, I

---

[4] Robinson, Haddon W., *Expository Preaching*, pp. 200-1.

think that there is some sense in occasionally watching a video recording of our preaching, in order to spot what gestures are unhelpful. I do not think we should do this more than about twice a year, in case we become too discouraged! But if modern technology can help us to improve as preachers, why shouldn't we reap its benefits?

[7] Your time

We end this chapter by considering an aspect of delivery that is often joked about, but which is nonetheless of great importance. It is the question of our time.

I want to remind us straightaway that we are not at the moment living through a great spiritual awakening. It is encouraging to see the continuing advance of the gospel throughout the world, but surely no one will pretend that we are experiencing anything like the Evangelical Awakening of the eighteenth century. During that period John Wesley, for example, often preached for two hours, and Jonathan Edwards for three! It was not unusual for men to preach several consecutive sermons. Their congregations remained gripped by the Word and lasting spiritual work was done.

Every preacher whom Christ has sent is aware that, left to himself, he can neither convert anybody nor do them any lasting good. He is grateful for everything that he knows of the Holy Spirit's help in expounding the Word and yet longs for that Spirit to come upon him in some unusual way. He knows that such an experience will be very different from a flow of adrenalin or the sense of elation that all speakers feel from time to time. He knows that he could well find himself preaching for hours on end. He also knows that in the meantime normal rules should apply!

The normal rules are these:

- Know what time is at your disposal.
- Start on time—don't reward persistent latecomers!
- End on time. People have come on the understanding that the meeting will last for a certain time. Finishing on time is therefore a question of integrity. It also causes you to be respected and so increases your usefulness.
- Don't take to yourself time that has been allocated to anyone who might be sharing the meeting with you. This has rightly been called 'platform robbery', because it involves taking from others what can never be restored to them.

It is always better to leave a congregation longing rather than loathing. We are not living in an age which, generally speaking, appreciates long sermons. You can't say much of substance in ten minutes, and most people today find forty minutes to be wearying.

However, some congregations, having been patiently educated to this, can listen for much longer than others. This is something for us to bear in mind when we are deciding how much material to present. Perhaps a good rule of thumb is to preach for about thirty minutes or slightly more, but to make it feel like twenty minutes,[5] for 'The true way to shorten a sermon is to make it more interesting' (H. W. Beecher).

When we have finished our sermon, we should *stop*! It is wrong to pad out a sermon just to make it fill up the allotted time. Why would a preacher do such a thing? Perhaps he does not want to be criticised for finishing too

---

[5] This piece of advice is based on Stott, John R. W., *I Believe in Preaching* (London, Hodder & Stoughton, 1982), p. 294.

soon; in this case his motive is entirely selfish and is not worthy of a Christian, let alone a herald of the Word. Or perhaps he does not want to disappoint the congregation; but he is more likely to disappoint people by inflicting on them unnecessary waffle than by being too brief.

Most preachers, however, have the opposite problem; they find it hard to finish on time! Nothing will cure them except a good dose of thoughtfulness for others. If they are running out of time they should edit what remains, finish at the moment expected, and then go home and repent for their inadequate preparation. Properly prepared preachers don't overrun.

Some men, conscious that they are running out of time, commit the sin of public dishonesty. They tell their hearers that they will soon be finished, and then go on and on. If you are a preacher like this, someone needs to ask you a blunt question: why should we now take to heart your message, seeing that we have heard with our own ears that you are a *liar*?

* * *

How important helpful delivery is! It is not a skill that we can learn in a day. If we are developing as preachers, we will be more and more conscious of how much progress we still have to make in this area. We will continue to read books on preaching, to attend lectures and conferences, and to seek help wherever we can get it. We will be attentive to the delivery of others, to see if there any tips that we can pick up. We will stop being bashful about asking friends and colleagues to comment on our own delivery.

But there is something that is more important than all of that; it is the ability to get out of our skin and to see and hear ourselves preach. We simply must learn to put ourselves in the shoes of those who hear us and to draw up our own objective evaluation of our delivery. As long as we live, we must do this *every time we preach*!

* * *

Something to do

1. Evaluate your own delivery and draw up a plan for improving it.

2. What, in your opinion, are the 'top ten sins' committed by those whose delivery is unhelpful? Write down your answer.

3. In what senses is all preaching *drama*, and how does this affect how it is to be done? Discuss this with some other preachers.

7
Supernatural Authority

In 1973 I made my first visit to the United States of America. During that time I spent several days with Pastor A. N. Martin of Trinity Baptist Church, Montville, New Jersey. Someone in his congregation gave me a booklet giving details of his recorded preaching, and in it was a comment which changed my life for ever. The booklet explained that Pastor Martin's sermons were characterised by 'exegetical accuracy, doctrinal substance, clear structure, vivid illustration, pointed application and spiritual urgency'. At last I had a checklist that told me about the ingredients that make up great preaching!

As you can see, although I have added a chapter on 'Helpful Delivery', I have made free use of that checklist while writing this book. You might have expected, then, that this final chapter would be called 'Spiritual Urgency'. But it is not, and here is the explanation.

A couple of chapters back I said that I would return to the subject of passion. That moment has now arrived. Much more needs to be said about the need for emotional engagement while preaching. I am writing this book in Great Britain at the beginning of the twenty-first century. I am living here at a time when a lot is being said and written about preaching, and countless courses are being organised to help people preach better. But I cannot hide my personal conviction that a lot of what is going on is more likely to ruin true preaching than to restore it.

The impression is being widely given that the preacher is doing well enough if he gives a clear explanation of his Scripture passage and applies it to the people in front of him. As long as he has made his biblical exposition clear and relevant, he has completely discharged his responsibility. He doesn't need to do anything else. The Word of God can now be left to do its own unique work.

If this idea gains ground and dominates, we will soon be attending the funeral of true preaching. Its body will remain (although it will soon rot), but its soul will be gone. That soul is made up of two elements which are so intertwined that it is impossible to separate them. 'Spiritual Urgency' is one of those elements; it refers to the fact that in giving God's Word, the preacher gives his very self—the message is clothed in the passion, earnestness, concern and emotion that are found in the most hidden depths of his being. The other element is 'Supernatural Authority'; only God can reveal God, and if the Holy Spirit does not take the message to those secret recesses that no human voice can reach, the biblical message—however well presented —can do no good at all.

If what I am saying seems strange to you, I would ask you to think about a block of flats where fire has broken out on the ground floor. There is still a little time, so you race up to the top floor to warn the people who live there. What you say to them is accurate; the building really is on fire (exegetical accuracy). You tell them that if they do not escape right away, they will perish in the flames (doctrinal substance). You express yourself clearly (clear structure, vivid illustration). You look them in the eyes and talk to them as individuals (pointed application, helpful delivery). But what if you did all this without expressing any urgency, either in your tone or in your manner? What if you said it all in a 'couldn't care less' way? Would you not seem to them like a practical joker? And how much success would your visit have?

Where there is no emotion, there is no persuasion. This is true in this world, and it is more than true in the spiritual dimension. Passionless preaching is not preaching at all. Not only so, but it is an insult to God, as Richard Baxter so often emphasised:

> What! Speak coldly for God, and for men's salvation? Can we believe that our people must be converted or condemned, and yet speak in a drowsy tone? In the name of God, brethren, labour to awaken your own hearts, before you go to the pulpit, that you may be fit to awaken the hearts of sinners. Remember they must be awakened or damned, and that a sleepy preacher will hardly awaken drowsy sinners. Though you give the holy things of God the highest praises in words, yet, if you do it coldly, you will seem by your manner to unsay what you said in the matter. It is a kind of contempt of great things, especially of so great things, to speak of them without much affection and fervency. The manner, as well as the words, must set them forth.[1]

Our need of the Spirit
But passion, on its own, cannot do spiritual work. This is true even when we are talking about the holy passion that floods from a godly man's heart. However sanctified it may be, it still has a human taste to it and so cannot perform a divine work. Only the Spirit can bring about a spiritual transformation. The best preaching in the world,

---

[1] Baxter, Richard, *The Reformed Pastor* (Edinburgh, The Banner of Truth Trust, 1974), p. 148.

without the Spirit's touch, is nothing. The Bible on its own, even when perfectly expounded, cannot do anything to anybody; its truth has got to be impressed on the human heart by its divine Author. Something heavenly has got to happen if the preacher is to speak with supernatural authority. If this does not happen, men and women will always receive the Word of God as if it were the word of *men* (see 1 Thessalonians 1:5, 2:13).

So how can I speak with spiritual urgency? And is there any road to speaking with supernatural authority? These are the questions to which we must now come.

Spiritual urgency

Spiritual urgency is the fruit of a single conviction. Where this gets hold of a man and masters him, he will not fail in this area. So what is that conviction? It is *that I have the truth that men and women need to hear*.

Do you believe that? Do you believe it really and deeply? Do you believe it not only when you are preaching evangelistically, but also when you are giving so-called 'teaching messages'? If you do, you will speak well enough, for this conviction is the mother of all true eloquence.

Preachers in the Bible spoke with spiritual urgency. They stood up and gave their message, knowing that they had the *truth* which people everywhere needed to take on board. 'I believed, therefore I spoke', says the psalmist (Psalm 116:10), and Paul and Timothy cry out their echo in writing, 'Since we have the same spirit of faith, according to what is written, "*I believed and therefore I spoke*", we also believe and therefore speak' (2 Corinthians 4:13). Peter and John, unveiling the heart of all the apostles, had said years earlier, 'We cannot but speak the things which we have seen and heard' (Acts 4:20). No wonder they spoke with such feeling! No wonder their preaching was so compelling! As I was told when I was a theological student, 'He who cannot *but* speak, will speak to people who cannot *but* hear!'

From the very moment you are convinced that you have the truth that everyone needs to hear, you will speak as a man in earnest. Your speech will be persuasive for, as Hywel Griffiths used to say, 'Only what comes from the heart will reach the heart.' The tone of your voice, the expression of your face and everything about your manner will combine together to arrest attention. The consciences of your hearers will tell them that they are listening to a man who believes what he is saying.

People everywhere are in danger of eternal hell. The unrepentant will go there, and so will every professing Christian who does not persevere in the faith. Nothing but the truth will rescue them. Nothing but the truth will cause them to grow in grace and in the knowledge of our Lord Jesus Christ. And you have that truth! If that conviction gets hold of you, you will never fail to rouse the men and women, teenagers and children who listen to you, despite all your flaws of content and presentation. Your urgency will come through. Different preachers will express this urgency in different ways, and even the same preacher will express it in different ways on different occasions. But your urgency will come through. The human spirit detects its presence and its ears prick up. But, let it be noted, the human spirit also detects its absence and, at that point, sinks into a slumber of indifference.

The great eighteenth-century evangelist, George Whitefield, knew about spiritual urgency. When polite congregations shuffled and whispered during his preaching, he stamped his foot, spoke to them forthrightly, and insisted on being heard. When hostile crowds resorted to every imaginable tactic to drown him out, he raised his voice and overcame them. He had the truth that they needed to be saved! He would not be silenced! Somehow or other, he would get his message into their ears! Yes, he would speak to them in plain words, using word-pictures that they could understand. Yes, he would make applications suitable to his hearers. But underlying everything was an all-conquering passion which drove him on, and which, under the Spirit's blessing, led to the conversion of tens of thousands.

Emotion

Why are we so afraid of emotion? As long as it is moved by truth, and *only* moved by truth, how can it be dangerous? Is, perhaps, the problem inside us? Are we scared of being accused of being 'beside ourselves' (see 2 Corinthians 5:13)? Are we resisting the spirit of our Lord, expressed in the psalmist's 'Zeal for your house has eaten me up' (John 2:17; see Psalm 69:9)? Are we distancing ourselves from the apostle Paul, whose 'spirit was provoked within him when he saw that the city was given over to idols' (Acts 17:16)? Have we become so hypocritical that we honour men like Daniel Rowland, but conveniently forget that he only ever preached 'as if on fire'?

It is said of one famous twentieth-century London preacher that he always left every one of his hearers soothed, comforted and at peace. This was the reason that people loved him so much. The Word of God calls us to turn our back on such preaching. It calls us to do away with smooth discourses which lull people into a false sense of security, or woo them into a deep sense of personal pleasure. It calls us to preach with conviction, fervour, energy and earnestness.

It scorns all pomp, display and pretended emotion, and instructs us to proclaim God's truth with deep feeling, anguish, warmth, life and love. Our calling is to pull down and to build up, to wound and to heal, to distress and to comfort, to weep, to yearn, to plead and to exhort. It is not enough to simply get the message right; we must be *in* that message, investing the whole of our being in its proclamation.

Many sermons today are as monotonous as the tolling of a funeral bell. The content is satisfactory, but the heart of the preacher is never seen. There is no risk that such preachers will ever be accused of false fire or fanaticism, because there is no evidence that any sort of flame is burning inside them. Where is the zeal and impassioned pleading of biblical preaching? Where is the weeping of the prophets and apostles? How many modern preachers could honestly say, 'I did not cease to warn everyone night and day with tears' (Acts 20:31)?

Let us go and hear Mr Average Evangelical preach in this twenty-first century. What seems to drive him is the desire to keep his hearers interested, rather than to see the living God glorified in their conversion and spiritual growth. For about half an hour he weaves together a biblical message which is mostly quite pleasant to listen to. But there is no way that it can be described as the most unforgettable event of the week! It doesn't shake anybody up, nor does it thrill them. All you can say about the sermon is that it was OK. No one's conscience has been stormed, and no one has wanted to cry out with sheer joy. Many of this week's television programmes have been infinitely more memorable than this explanation of God's truth!

What a disgrace! We who preach must seek God out and confess to him our extreme depravity. Great thoughts do not engage our minds completely. Again and again we have managed to preach *truth* coldly and feebly. We have looked lost people in the eyes and have left them without pleading with them or giving ourselves to sustained persuasion. The whole of our heart has not always been in everything we say. We have often come across as less than serious, and sometimes even as light. Our hearts are hard. We must admit that the old preacher got it right: 'It is because there is so much hard-heartedness in the pulpit that there is still so much in the pew.' Thank God that in Christ there is forgiveness for men like us!

Supernatural authority

Supernatural authority is experienced by preachers who have been mastered by a single conviction. Where this gets hold of a man and governs the whole of his ministry, he cannot fail to know something of this glorious blessing. So what is that conviction? It is *that the message I am preaching can do no good to anyone unless it is accompanied by the Spirit of God.*

No message can accomplish anything unless God blesses it. We can sow the seed, we can even water it, but only God can give it life (1 Corinthians 3:6). If we preach faithfully, but do not see any conversions, what is the explanation? If we open up the Word, but do not see believers transformed by our messages, how shall we account for it? The answer is always that God has held back his power. He has not done what only he can do.

No spiritual work can be done where God's Spirit is not at work. Preaching will always fail unless God himself works through it. Isaiah understood this: 'Who has believed our report? And to whom has the arm of the LORD been revealed?', he cried (Isaiah 53:1). His two questions are in fact one, and yet the second one contains the answer to the first—if anyone at all has believed, it is because the arm of the Lord has been revealed to him; but if someone has *not* believed, it is because the arm of the Lord has *not* been revealed to him. No one can believe unless God visits their heart in mighty power. Not even a display of miracles can bring them to that point (see John 12:37-38). Something must go on *inside* them, and that is something that only God can bring about.

Our Lord himself taught this lesson in the plainest possible way. It was a lesson that many of his disciples refused to accept, and from the moment they heard it they turned their back on him (John 6:66). Those who accepted the lesson continued with him. They had learned the most basic secret of the Christian ministry. Our Lord's exact words were, 'No one can come to me unless the Father who sent me draws him . . . no one can come to me unless it has been granted to him by my Father' (John 6:44,65). If God himself is not at work, there is nothing that we can do that can bring a single person to Christ. We have simply *got* to have his blessing as we preach!

Richard Cecil learned this lesson quite early in his ministry, and went on to become one of the most powerful preachers of the eighteenth-century Evangelical Awakening in Britain. Here is his testimony:

I once said to myself in the foolishness of my heart, 'What sort of a sermon must that have been, which was preached by St. Peter, when three thousand souls were converted at once!' What sort of sermon! Such as other sermons. There is nothing to be found in it extraordinary. The effect was not produced by his eloquence, but by the mighty power of God present with his Word. It is in vain to attend one Minister after another and to have sermon after sermon, unless we pray that the Holy Spirit may accompany his Word.[2]

God uses men to advance his cause, and yet it is always to God that all advance must be attributed. How is it that those first witnesses in Syrian Antioch had such success? 'The hand of the Lord was with them, and a great number believed and turned to the Lord' (Acts 11:21). Why was Lydia the only convert in that Philippian riverside prayer meeting? 'The Lord opened her heart to heed the things spoken by Paul' (Acts 16:14). How can we explain the instant conversion of dozens of pagans and Jews in Thessalonica?

Our gospel did not come to you in word only, but also in power, and in the Holy Spirit, and in much assurance . . . For this reason we also thank God without ceasing, because when you received the word of God which you heard from us, you welcomed it not as the word of men, but as it is in truth, the word of God, which also effectively works in you who believe.

(1 Thessalonians 1:5; 2:13)

With God all things are possible. Without him, nothing is possible. Two thousand years of church history reveal that it is not enough to be a preacher who is highly gifted or technically perfect, although neither gift nor hard work is to be despised. Many men of modest gift have been used to transform whole communities, and sometimes nations.

[2] Quoted by Bridges, Charles, in *The Christian Ministry* (London, The Banner of Truth Trust, 1958), p. 79.

On occasions a single sentence has conquered the gospel's enemies in situations where all arguments have failed. Sometimes the Word comes with power and sometimes it does not. In preaching, then, we should not rely on the quality of our preparation and presentation, however important these may be. We must rely only on God, and we must never adopt any approach which minimises our dependence on him.

Paul provides us with the right approach as he describes his ministry in Corinth:

> And I, brethren, when I came to you, did not come with excellence of speech or of wisdom declaring to you the testimony of God. For I determined not to know anything among you except Jesus Christ and him crucified. I was with you in weakness, in fear, and in much trembling. And my speech and my preaching were not with persuasive words of human wisdom, but in demonstration of the Spirit and of power, that your faith should not be in the wisdom of men but in the power of God.
>
> (1 Corinthians 2:1-5)

Unction

In 1961 I came across a little book which I have read at least once a year ever since. It was called *Power Through Prayer* by E. M. Bounds.[3] Next to the Bible and the Westminster Shorter Catechism, I can say that this book has had more influence on me than any other book I have read. As I worked through the book I arrived at the chapter whose title is 'Under the Dew of Heaven'. There I read

---

[3] Bounds, E. M., *Power Through Prayer*, World-wide Circulation Edition (London Marshall, Morgan & Scott, undated). All the quotations are from chapter 10, pp. 43ff.

things that mystified me. They were beyond my experience. I simply could not understand what the writer was talking about. Here are a few examples:

Unction is that indefinable, indescribable something which an old, renowned Scottish preacher describes thus: 'There is sometimes somewhat in preaching that cannot be described either to matter or expression, and cannot be described what it is, or from whence it cometh, but with a sweet violence it pierceth into the heart and affections and comes immediately from the Lord; but if there be any way to obtain such a thing it is by the heavenly disposition of the speaker' . . .

This divine unction is the feature which separates and distinguishes true gospel preaching from all other methods of presenting the truth, and which creates a wide spiritual chasm between the preacher who has it and the one who has it not. It supports and impregnates revealed truth with all the energy of God. Unction is simply putting God in His own Word and on His own preacher . . . Enlargement, freedom, fullness of thought, directness and simplicity of utterance are the fruits of this unction . . .

This unction is the one divine enablement by which the preacher accomplishes the peculiar and saving ends of preaching. Without this unction there are no spiritual results accomplished; the results and forces in preaching do not rise above the results of unsanctified speech. Without unction the former is as potent as the pulpit . . .

It is the presence of this unction on the preacher that creates the stir and friction in many a congregation. The same truths have been told in the strictness of the letter, but no ruffle has been seen, no pain or pulsation felt. All is quiet as a graveyard. Another preacher comes, and this mysterious influence is on him: the letter of the Word has been fired by the Spirit, the throes of a mighty movement are felt, it is the unction that pervades and stirs the conscience and breaks the heart. Unctionless preaching makes everything hard, dry, acrid, dead.

Unction? Even today I am not convinced that this word is the right one to describe what Dr Bounds was talking about. But what *was* he talking about?—that was my question. At that stage in my life I had had no experience of this phenomenon, either in my own life or the life of anyone else. I simply could not imagine what the author had in mind.

During the spring of the next year I sensed that things were soon going to change. I was a student at the time and my mother telephoned me, asking me if I could come home. There was a man she wanted me to meet. He was a man in his mid-sixties who had once been a coalminer but who had now been a minister for over twenty-five years. He was preaching at a week of meetings in our village, and there was something about him that she could not put into words. I would understand if I could hear him for myself. All she could tell me was that it was wonderful.

It was impossible for me to go home and I had to wait another year before I heard Hywel Griffiths preach. As I sat in the pews of Cosheston Mission Church, I understood at last what 'unction' was. The preacher's sermons were quite lengthy, filled with word-pictures and delivered with obvious love and deep emotion. But there was something else. They were accompanied by an indefinable influence. As Hywel Griffiths preached, heaven came to earth. The invisible world was more real than the visible one. There was a touch of glory. Christ was more precious than any-thing or anyone in the universe. The Word came over with a self-authenticating force that was irresistible. Not to believe was not an option, because it was indescribably foolish. The only wise thing to do was to trust the Lord completely, and to love him with all of my heart, soul, mind and strength.

I was not alone in receiving these impressions. After each sermon the congregation sat in stunned silence, overcome by the sheer power of the Word. Sometimes the silence was followed by spontaneous prayer. Some came to Christ. Many others like me, who were already believers, were changed for ever. We had experienced a small taste of what happens in revival, and we all knew now what 'unction' was. I would never have any more trouble understanding what E. M. Bounds was writing about!

> The unction, the divine unction, this heavenly anointing, is what the pulpit needs and must have. This divine and heav-enly oil put on it by the imposition of God's hand must soften and lubricate the whole man—heart, head, spirit—until it separates him with a mighty separation from all earthly, secular, worldly, selfish motives and aims, sepa-rating him to everything that is pure and Godlike.

Obtaining unction

So how is unction obtained? I am glad to tell you that I know the answer, not only from my reading, but also from my own experience. We cannot command the Spirit of God. The heavenly wind blows wherever it wishes (John 3:8). We don't even know where it has just been or where it will go to next. We have no control over it whatever. God is God and he does whatever he pleases (Psalm

115:3; 135:6). He will never bind himself to do the will of a man.

And yet God answers prayer. He does! He does it because he has promised to do it. It is to saved sinners that he makes the pledge, 'And all things, whatever you ask in prayer, believing, you will receive' (Matthew 21:22). It is into the hands of saved sinners that he puts strong arguments to use in prayer: 'If you then, being evil, know how to give good gifts to your children, how much more will your Father who is in heaven give good things to those who ask him!' (Matthew 7:11). It is to saved sinners that his Son gives the extraordinary invitation, 'And whatever you ask in my name, that I will do, that the Father may be glorified in the Son. If you ask anything in my name, I will do it' (John 14:13-14). And these three extracts are only a sample. We all know that there are dozens of similar promises scattered throughout the Bible.

It is the duty of every believer, and therefore every preacher, to drop from his life everything that grieves the Holy Spirit (Ephesians 4:30). It is the calling of Christian preachers to proclaim Christ, knowing that the Spirit loves to glorify him and so is likely to bless such preaching (John 16:14). But the finest summary of the preacher's priorities is that drawn up by the apostles during the infancy of the Christian church: 'We will give ourselves continually to prayer and to the ministry of the Word' (Acts 6:4)—in that order!

There is such a thing as conquering God. It is possible to so labour in prayer, and to so lay hold of God in the secret place, that you receive from him a personal assurance that he is going to supernaturally accompany you when you preach. It is possible to so wrestle and writhe and sweat in prayer that you leave the place of prayer both

161

in peace and exhausted, sure in your heart that the Lord himself is going to bless your next message and to accompany you wonderfully as you preach it. This does not mean that it is possible to *earn* God's blessing. It does not mean that there are any *works* we can offer him, for which he is obliged to reward us. It simply means that in his grace he allows himself to be conquered by importunate prayer.

Do you believe that? Do you believe that a man can say to his God, 'I will not let you go unless you bless me' (Genesis 32:26)? Do you believe that it can be said of such a man that the Lord 'blessed him there' (Genesis 32:29)? If you do not, how will you ever understand the ministry of men like John Chrysostom, Martin Luther, John Wesley, Jonathan Edwards, Daniel Rowland, John Elias, C .H. Spurgeon, Hywel Griffiths, D. Martyn Lloyd-Jones—and Hugh Morgan? These men were very different from each other and preached in very different situations, so what did they have in common? They relied on God, and they relied on him completely. So they set themselves to seek him, to find him, to know him, to conquer him and to experience his blessing. They were not primarily preachers; they were men of prayer. And on the occasions they prayed as usual, but saw God hold back his blessing, they were content to whisper, 'Even so, Father, for so it seemed good in your sight' (Matthew 11:26).

E. M. Bounds understood:

How and whence comes this unction? Direct from God in answer to prayer. Praying hearts only are the hearts filled with this holy oil; praying lips only are anointed with this divine unction.

Prayer, much prayer, is the price of preaching unction; prayer, much prayer, is the one, sole condition of keeping this unction. Without unceasing prayer the unction never comes to the preacher. Without perseverance in prayer the unction, like the manna overkept, breeds worms.

* * *

The main part of this modest book has now come to an end. I have tried to show you what preaching is and what are its essential ingredients. I want to thank you for reading this far. I also want to encourage you to read what remains.

I believe that everything I have said is important. If any of its chapters were dropped, I believe that this book would be both defective and unbalanced. But if you pressed me to tell you which chapters I consider to be of particular importance at this hour, I would undoubtedly point you to the chapters on Exegetical Accuracy and Supernatural Authority. This is because of my convictions about our need of both Word and Spirit.

I am 62 years old and I trust that the Lord will still give me a few more years of ministry. Be that as it may, I am conscious that I am nearer to the end of my life than its beginning. My special prayer, then, is that a whole cohort of younger men will get particular help from this book and will give themselves to doing what it says, at least as far as it is line with Scripture. And may their ministries be a blessing to the whole world!

> My talents, gifts, and graces, Lord,
>   Into Thy blessèd hands receive;
> And let me live to preach Thy Word,
>   And let me to Thy glory live;
> My every sacred moment spend
> In publishing the sinners' Friend.
>   *Charles Wesley, 1707–88*

* * *

Something to do

1. You feel so deeply about what you preach that you have become a ranter. Fortunately your wife tells you about it. What are you going to do?

2. Explain to an interested young Christian what Evangelicals, historically, have meant by the term 'unction'.

3. Explore the connection between prayer and 'unction'.

PART THREE

1
A suggested method of sermon preparation

2
Remembered with affection:
HUGH DAVID MORGAN
(1928–1992)

1

A suggested method of
sermon preparation

Sermons need preparing. 'Habitually to come into the pulpit unprepared is unpardonable presumption', said C. H. Spurgeon.[1] John Stott reminds us of another point: 'The great preachers who have influenced their generation have all borne witness to the need for conscientious preparation.'[2]

Preaching is the means that God uses to awaken the dead and to build up the living. If we believe that, we will not dare to approach it in any other way except prayerfully, seriously and studiously. Our preaching *gift* comes from God; our *development* of that gift is our responsibility.

The lawyer carefully prepares his brief; the architect draws up his plans; the doctor studies both his case notes and the patient—and will I, a preacher of the gospel, go to *the most important work in the world* in a slipshod way?

Despite the excellent example given to us in Ecclesiastes 12:9-12, there are no hard and fast rules for sermon preparation. What follows is a personal method that I would like to commend to you, especially if you have only recently begun to preach. It covers all the essentials, and marries sermon preparation to prayer. It is not intended to

---

[1] Spurgeon, C. H., *Lectures to My Students*, Second Series (London, Passmore & Alabaster, 1882), p. 4.
[2] Stott, John R. W., *I Believe in Preaching* (London, Hodder & Stoughton, 1982), p. 212.

be a rule, but a guide. You will probably want to alter it, or to depart from it, at certain points. Nonetheless I am quite sure that some men will find it helpful.

Ten steps to effective preaching

- Start your preparation as early as possible. Hurried preparation is bad preparation.
- To keep putting it off is to invite failure—God does not work unnecessary miracles in order to make up for the laziness of the preacher.
- The essential thing is to *get started*—don't *think* about it —*do* it!
- Sit down at a large table/desk, on a hard chair, with plenty of light, your Bible to hand, with a pencil and plenty of paper.
- And follow this step-by-step guide, *never* going on to the next step before fully completing the previous one.

1. Reflect on your task

- Stop!
- Be absolutely silent in the presence of the Lord.
- Take time to call to mind what your task is. You are to glorify God by changing unbelievers into believers, and weak Christians into strong ones.
- It is true that this is done by the exposition and application of the Word of God. You are, however, not primarily a maker of *sermons*, but a maker of *saints*.
- It is essential that you do not lose sight of this throughout your preparation.

2. Meditate on your text

- By the word 'text' we mean the part of Scripture on which you are to preach, be it a verse, several verses, a paragraph, a chapter, a book, a biblical theme . . .
- How you select your text is not something we have dealt with in this book, but you can easily find helpful advice on this subject in other books on preaching.

- ***On your knees (literally!)***. Now read your text.
- Take it sentence by sentence, word by word, using every part as fuel for prayer.
- Yes—concentrate on the text to the exclusion of everything else; avoid all (*all!*) interruptions; brood on the text in the Lord's presence.
- Worship him for every truth and lesson that you see.
- If there is any part of your text that you do not understand, pray, brood and meditate until you do. If light still does not come, consult your commentaries and other aids—but only to find out what this phrase or sentence means, and nothing more.

- As you wait upon God, thoughts will begin to come, perhaps slowly at first. But one thought will suggest another, and this in turn will lead to another.
- Stay on your knees until the passage inflames your soul—until the fire burns, making you impatient to preach the truths which you have now made your own, and especially the 'big idea', that is, the dominant thought which sums up what the text is about.
- You have not asked for a message. But the Word of God is now enthusing you and the direction of your message is clear.

3. Begin to write

- *Go to your desk* and ask your text questions. Write down the answers. Don't try at this stage to arrange anything into any logical sequence—this can be done later. *Take time* to do this work thoroughly— paper is not in short supply and you can use lots of it, if necessary.

- First of all, ask these basic questions:

  * What is the immediate, wider and historical context?

  * What did this text mean to the author and to the original hearers? And what does it have to say today?

  * What does it teach about God, the Father, the Son, the Holy Spirit?

  * What does it teach about men, their attitude to God and to each other?

  * Is there a good example to follow, or a bad one to avoid?

  * Is there a command to obey?

  * Is there a warning to heed?

  * Is there a promise to believe and proclaim?

  * Is there an answer to a biblical or personal question?

  * Is there some teaching to take particularly to heart?

  * Is there a teaching confirmed by other passages of the Bible?

- Now ask *some other questions*: for example, those found in Haddon W. Robinson, chapter 4 (*Expository Preaching*, Leicester, IVP, 1986), *Search the Scriptures* (Leicester, IVP, 1967) and *This Morning With God* (Downers Grove, InterVarsity Press, 1968).

4. Arrange your material

- Still in an attitude of prayer, it is time to write down *in rough* a first draft of your sermon notes. This will mean working through the several pieces of paper you have already filled, improving what is there, and adding the new thoughts which will certainly suggest themselves.

- Start by getting a fresh piece of paper and writing down *why* you are preaching this message. What is its *purpose*? State this in one phrase.

- Now decide what *form* the sermon must take for this purpose to be fulfilled. For example, do you have an idea to explain? a proposition to prove? a principle to apply? a story to tell? a subject to complete? or what?

- Leave a gap for the *Introduction*, which you will put in later.
- Divide your paper into three columns, labelling them *State*, *Illustrate*, *Apply*.
- In the column labelled *State* write down the message that you are going to bring from the text. Do nothing until the structure is clear, simple, natural—a structure supplied by the text itself. Then fill it in.
- Refuse to write a full manuscript. Write one thought per line.
- Keep to the point. Discard everything that does not serve the 'big idea'.

- For every major truth written down, find or invent an illustration. Write it against that truth in the column labelled *Illustrate*.
- Visualising the people to whom you will preach, write down in the column labelled *Apply* an application

171

against every major truth taught and illustrated. It will help to subdivide this column into *What* (to do), *How* (to do it), *Why* (it should be done).

• When you have finished your rough notes, each of the three columns should be almost equally full.

• This done, now insert an *Introduction* into the space you have left. It must whet the appetite and lead your hearers into the subject of the sermon.

• Finally, prepare a *Conclusion* to the message. Keep something up your sleeve that you can fire into their hearts, so as to persuade your hearers to take action concerning the text's 'big idea'. It is time for holy violence!

5. Work through your checklist

• Rework your rough notes, dropping or adding material as necessary in the light of the following checklist. Don't skimp this vitally important part of your preparation. *Take time*.

1. ***Exegetical accuracy***. Does this message really grasp and convey *the intended meaning* of the text, majoring on its dominant thought ('the big idea') and driving it home? If the exegesis is sound, the message will all the time be drawing attention to the Lord Jesus Christ and his cross (Luke 24:27; Acts 3:24). Use commentaries and lexical aids to check out this point.

2. ***Doctrinal substance***. In what specific ways will this message advance people's understanding of that *system* of doctrine that the Holy Scriptures teach? Check any doctrinal points against the historic confessions of the

Christian church (for example, the Westminster or London Confessions) to make sure that there is no doctrinal error or imbalance.

3. *Clear structure*. You have lived with this material for some time, but the congregation will hear it only once. Is the structure of the message obvious, crystal-clear and easy to follow? As a general rule, have only three or four headings, and no subheadings. Does everything serve the dominant thought? Is the intro-duction brief, interesting, arresting, and the servant of what follows? Does the conclusion encapsulate the message and insist on a verdict?

4. *Vivid illustration*. Do the illustrations comprise one-third of the message? Do they really serve the truths which are to be explained, or the applications which are to be made? Drop all illustrations which draw attention to yourself.

5. *Pointed application*. Are there applications for *every* truth to be explained? Do they comprise one-third of the message? Are they really relevant to the people to whom you will preach? Are they expressed kindly?

6. Write up your notes

- Write up your sermon notes for best.
- Take time and trouble in getting your language *just right*. Make it concrete and plain, accurate and vivid. Choose words which are simple and clear—most of them should have only one or two syllables. Keep your sentences brief, each one containing a single thought. Use the second person wherever possible ('you').

- Be sure that you have included *lots and lots* of rhetorical questions.
- Consider where it would be helpful to engage in repetition.

- In preparing your notes, aim above all for clarity. They must be *easy* to read.
- Write large—or type.
- Write on one side of the paper only.
- Number the pages.
- Underline in red the main headings, and, if there have to be subheadings, underline these in blue or green.

7. Deal with your God

- On your knees again, to pray over the completed notes. This is a million times better than rehearsing your message!
- The *first* time, pray over every line, asking that it will draw people's attention to the Triune God, causing them to think great thoughts about him.
- The *second* time, pray over every line, asking that it might bring the unconverted to Christ, and may advance the converted in both grace and knowledge.
- This time of prayer may move you to make certain alterations to your completed notes. Don't hesitate to do this. Your notes are neither sacred nor infallible.

- Remain on your knees: choose the psalms and hymns, and arrange all the other details of the order of service.
- The service should be a whole. Everything in it should serve and underline the dominant thought (or 'big idea') to be proclaimed in the message.

8. Make final preparations

- Arrive at the church early.

- Go into the pulpit, or on to the platform, and acquaint yourself with the lectern, the amplification, the seating, and with all the physical circumstances connected with your preaching.

- Arrange your Bible, notes, order of service and hymn book well before the service starts.

- Greet as many of the people as you can and, if possible, have a time of prayer with the church officers before the service begins.

9. Go to your work

- God's providence has appointed *you* to lead and preach today—so do it, with prayerfulness, authority and love.

- Look your congregation in the eyes and speak out.

- Concentrate on two things only—lifting up the Lord, and making these people into saints. The service and the preaching are only means to these great ends. They must never become ends in themselves.

10. Hide away in secret

- Sometime afterwards, find a quiet place to have a sustained time of private prayer.

- Bring out once more your order of service and sermon notes, and pray over them.

- Ask for forgiveness for every point where you could have done better.

- Pray for every truth announced—that the people might call them to mind—that this will cause them to have great thoughts about God—that the unsaved will be converted—that the converted may make significant progress both in spiritual understanding and living.

- Pray for as many specific individuals as you can remember.

- And then leave everything in the Lord's hands—and start preparing the next message!

* * *

How long will it normally take to prepare a sermon in a living situation? The answer is: *as long as it takes*! Who can tell how quickly it will all come together, and how long it might take to wrestle with God in prayer until you have a personal assurance that he is going to bless this particular sermon on this particular occasion?

This much we can say: in order to prepare a thirty-minute sermon you will need at least twelve hours to begin with. This may, and probably will, get less as the years go by. The minimum you are likely to get down to is one hour of preparation for every five minutes preached.

My suggested method emphasises that sermons are not an end in themselves. They are simply a *means* by which God is glorified in the building up of believers and the conversion of unbelievers. The method encourages unhurried meditation on the text, unashamed commitment to doctrinal purity, sustained effort to produce a clear structure, diligent preparation of illustrations and applications, constant review in the light of defined criteria, close attention to note-writing, persevering prayer, bold proclamation and personal repentance.

If you follow this method, your sermon preparation will never be hasty and will include every element required for great preaching. And isn't such preaching the obvious need of the hour?

Hugh D. Morgan

2
Remembered with affection:
Hugh David Morgan (1928–1992)

This is a book on preaching, so why is it closing with a tribute to a greatly missed gospel minister? The answer is simple: there have not been too many modern preachers who have exemplified the principles set out in the preceding pages. But there have been some, and Hugh Morgan was one of them. Although he has now been in glory for several years, his influence remains. He was a man of God who gave living proof that what you have read so far can be put into practice, and that it can be combined with an active and caring pastoral ministry. In that way he continues to encourage us all.

His life

Hugh David Morgan was born in Llanelli in 1928, and was born again in the same town in 1945 during a wonderfully blessed week of evangelistic meetings taken by visiting students, in the course of which over one hundred young people were converted. It was during that week that he met Mari Williams whom he was later to marry. On leaving school he did two years of national service in the Royal Air Force before proceeding to Aberystwyth, and then Bala, to train for the ministry of the Presbyterian Church of Wales—originally known as the Calvinistic Methodist Connexion.

Hugh's first pastorate was in the Rhondda Valley, where he went in July 1953, just before his wedding to Mari. He stayed there nine years. The pastorate was composed of two churches, Bethany in Ton Pentre (where the young couple lived) and Duffryn in Gelli. Hugh found himself in a very difficult situation. The churches were soaked in years of liberal theology; most of the members, although religious, were unconverted; and church life was filled with concerts and sales of work which were relied on to raise funds. But the Lord had his hand on his young servant. He opened the Bible and boldly preached the gospel, doing so with meekness and overflowing love. Little by little resentment died down, enemies were conquered, hearts melted and numbers of people were awakened and saved. When the time came for Hugh and Mari and their daughters Bethan and Sian to move on, they did so as a family which was surrounded by the affection of their people.

In 1962 Hugh began his ministry at Malpas Road Presbyterian Church, Newport. It was a much larger church, but in recent years it had known very little of the gospel. From its pulpit Hugh began to systematically expound the Scriptures, seeing himself, however, not so much as a Bible teacher but as an evangelist. Behind his pulpit ministry lay a life of secret prayer, and married to it was the practical caring ministry which he and Mari exercised among their people throughout the week. The early years were very difficult and a number of people left the church. The period 1970–1980, however, was a time of exceptional blessing. In his preaching Hugh often had the impression that he was simply standing back, watching the Holy Spirit at work. Many people came to the Lord, while the church embraced the Evangelical Reformed faith and became a beacon for the gospel. It was this commitment to

the gospel which eventually led to the congregation seced-
ing from the denomination in 1976 and continuing as
Malpas Road Evangelical Church.

Hugh's thirty-nine years of ministry were not, however,
restricted to his two pastorates. He was deeply aware that the
cause of Christ was much bigger than his local situation.
From the very beginning he was a frequent open-air
preacher and an active participant in many missions to
students. In 1962 he became a member of the General
Committee of the Evangelical Movement of Wales, and
remained on it until his death! He was a leading figure in the
Movement's work among ministers, chaired its Finance
Committee, and chaired its General Committee during the
difficult days that followed a fire at Bryntirion, the
Movement's office and conference centre. He became
known across Wales, and well beyond, as a preacher of the
gospel and conference speaker. He lectured at the South
Wales Bible College in Barry, and continued to do so when
it was incorporated into the Evangelical Theological College
of Wales in Bridgend. He was committed to the work of the
Universities' and Colleges' Christian Fellowship, to the
monthly paper *Evangelicals Now*, and to the Associating
Evangelical Churches of Wales which, with others, he was
instrumental in forming. And we have not mentioned the
countless numbers of individual men and women whom he
advised and encouraged in so many ways. Hugh Morgan
was, quite simply, tireless in the work of the gospel.

One of Hugh Morgan's favourite Bible verses was
Philippians 1:21: 'For to me, to live is Christ, and to die is
gain.' On Thursday 30 January 1992 he spent most of the
day in Aberystwyth participating in the General
Committee of the Evangelical Movement of Wales. On
Friday 31 January he prepared for his preaching, engaged

in pastoral work and spent the evening with the elders of Malpas Road Evangelical Church discussing, among other things, preparations for the calling of a successor to the pastorate there. On Saturday 1 February 1992 at 7.00 a.m. he was taking part in his church's weekly prayer meeting for revival, and shortly after 9.00 a.m., after returning home, he was safely with his Lord in glory.

His character

There was a certain dignity, but nothing stuffy, about Hugh Morgan. Although he would say, 'I often pray, "Lord, make me as holy as a pardoned sinner can be"', he understood what true holiness was. It meant being serious about the things of God and disciplined in personal habits, but it did not mean being joyless or artificial. And so it was that he was a man of good humour, a lover of practical jokes, a player and spectator of rugby, and an avid reader of books and newspapers. Although he was a self-effacing man, people loved being near him; and this was especially true of his wife, his children and his grandchildren. Those who welcomed him into their homes as a visiting preacher, whether they were adults or children, longed for him to return.

He was a man of prayer. He did not find private prayer easy, but gave himself to it anyway. Often he prayed with fasting. He prayed as a student, he prayed as a minister, he prayed with his family and he prayed with his friends. He prayed for gospel work to be put into his hands and he prayed for both grace and strength to do it. He prayed for his people, he prayed for the church universal, and he had a particular burden to pray that the Lord would accompany the preached Word and that he would visit his people again in revival blessing.

He loved people, and especially the people whom the Lord had called him to pastor. These he served day and night, giving himself to them without any thought for his personal health or ease. He approached people with a hearty greeting and his winsome smile, and had no difficulty having sustained conversations with adults and children of any age or background. To him the greatest privilege in the world was to belong to the family of God, and his great desire was to see other people coming into that family. He did not, then, shirk from asking them blunt questions about their spiritual state, but did so without any hint of arrogance or insensitivity.

The last time I had a few hours with him was in a small town in northern Italy. He and Mari were on holiday in Switzerland and we travelled across the border for the day. We talked at length about the Reformation and its influence on the region, and Hugh was very insistent that we should visit the local Waldensian chapel. The pastor was having his siesta, but Hugh knocked gently at his door until he agreed to get up and show us around. The pastor knew very little English and Hugh knew no Italian, and yet somehow they managed to have a long conversation together. Quite soon it became clear that the man did not understand the gospel and had never experienced the new birth. It was wonderful to see how Hugh took the opportunity to quietly mention everything that the pastor needed to know to get safely from earth to heaven.

Hugh Morgan was always the same. His integrity was above reproach, his character was transparent, his manner was kind, and he was renowned for his gentleness and wisdom. His chief concern was always to do what pleased the Lord. When he was sure what that was, nothing could move him from doing it! Whatever the obstacles, however great the opposition, he would steadily and lovingly move along the right path, even if it meant going very slowly. Nothing could deter him. He did not know how to give up. There was no circle of people that he was trying to please; he was only interested in pleasing One.

His preaching

Those who never heard Hugh Morgan preach do not need to guess what his preaching is like because plenty of his recorded messages are still available from Malpas Road Evangelical Church, Newport. There is, however, a great difference between hearing someone on tape and hearing him in the flesh.

He knew his Bible well and spent most of his ministry expounding it systematically and thematically. He was careful with the text. He knew that he was handling the oracles of the living God and was deeply conscious of his responsibility not to distort their meaning. His preaching was wonderfully Christ-centred, and constantly brought into focus the great saving truths of the gospel. He was also concerned that the church of Jesus Christ, and therefore the men and women who compose it, should be holy. Holiness of heart and life, therefore, came across as a constant theme.

He was aware that he was preaching to ordinary people. Although his own understanding of the things of God became fuller and more refined with the years, his sermons remained both accessible and memorable. His own life and those of his people were closely interwoven and he was able therefore to speak right into their lives. This made his preaching relevant, direct and searching, with a decidedly contemporary note.

We can best describe Hugh Morgan's sermons as wonderful examples of *pastoral preaching*. He never cheapened or debased the Christian pulpit, but his manner was not formal or distant. He loved his people and they knew it. They knew it even when his reprimands were blunt and searching, because he spoke as a warm-hearted and gentle pastor and not as a censorious critic.

In giving his messages he also gave himself. His whole person was in what he had to say. This was seen in the way his body moved, in his facial expressions, and in the liveliness and passion of his delivery. But the discipline of his life and his insistence on serving the text meant that he never sank into that lack of restraint that is rightly viewed as fanaticism.

There was, then, no inconsistency or tension between his day-to-day life as a man of God, his pastoral ministry, and his public preaching. We admire the grace of God in him and see him as a model for Christian ministers for all generations. Such Christ-centred, all-rounded wholesomeness is not only impressive; it is unforgettable.

His legacy

Hugh Morgan's principal legacy to us lies, no doubt, in the example that he has left us, the chief features of which I have tried to outline above. However, as Christians at the beginning of this twenty-first century, there are a number of other lessons that we can learn from him.

His call to personal holiness remains valid and important for all time. An unholy life always brings disgrace upon the gospel that it professes. Hugh's four addresses to the English-speaking Aberystwyth Conference in 1978 are a moving blend of clear biblical teaching, impeccable doctrine and practical help. Published under the title *The Holiness of God and of His People*,[1] they should really always be in print. They have moved many to seek after the Lord in a new way.

In addition, Hugh understood that during the period of his ministry, the times had changed quite a lot. He had begun both his pastorates by setting out to evangelise the many people who came to chapel but who remained unconverted. As the years passed he noticed that the old chapel culture was passing too. Most people no longer had any connection with a place of worship. A new generation had grown up without any contact with the gospel. Were these people to be left to perish? Did not our evangelism now need to focus mostly on the people outside, rather than on the few inside? Was it not time to take new initiatives? What could be done to stir both churches and individual believers to bring the gospel to every person in our nation? And could we not remember to take nothing for granted and to speak to them in the simplest possible way? These were the questions that Hugh Morgan began increasingly to ask, and which, in private and public, he sought increasingly to address.

Hugh also felt compelled to encourage more reflection on the nature, calling and needs of the church. It is not right that congregations committed to the gospel should remain in church fellowship with bodies that oppose that gospel. On the other hand, it is not right that gospel churches should hold back in expressing their fellowship with each other, whether they are in the same body or not. These

---

[1] Bryntirion, Evangelical Press of Wales (now Bryntirion Press), 1979; third edition, revised and expanded, entitled *Holy God, holy people* (Bryntirion Press), 2007.

were the convictions that led Malpas Road Church to secede from its denomination. These were the convictions that moved Hugh to be one of those men instrumental in founding the Associating Evangelical Churches of Wales, as well as continuing to love and support gospel ministers and churches within mainline denominations, or elsewhere. Such churches and ministers must be *active* in promoting and expressing unity among gospel churches. Inertia will not do. It is a contradiction of biblical obedience.

Hugh was not blind to the tensions that existed among Evangelical Christians of various groupings in Wales. He did as much as he could to encourage the Lord's people to embrace each other. He was driven by his belief that it was wrong of them to see themselves as *separate* entities. They were one people. They belonged to each other. They needed each other. They should, therefore, love each other, meet up with each other, and work together in every way possible. This would encourage them all and would also be a good witness to the watching world. It has got to be done! And there must be no delay!

The lost multitudes, and the church's unholiness and disunity, underlined in Hugh's mind that the greatest need in any generation is that the Lord would visit his people with a pouring out of the Holy Spirit. We need revival. Yes, while waiting and praying for such a blessing we must give ourselves to evangelism, to building gospel churches and to encouraging the Lord's people everywhere. But we need revival. The days are desperate. Without a display of the Lord's power through the preached Word, how will we ever win our nation for Christ? How will we ever be the people we should be? We must plead with God to work among us in an exceptional way. We must lay hold of him. We must not let him go until he blesses us. We must pray, and we must pray together. We must never give up.

Hugh Morgan has gone from us, but his legacy remains. How can we benefit from this legacy if we don't know anything about it? My prayer is that this short tribute will help to bring it back to our attention, to show us that we ignore it at our peril, and to assure us that the door of blessing remains open to those who take it to heart.

> From heavenly Jerusalem's towers,
>   The path through the desert they trace;
> And every affliction they suffered
>   Redounds to the glory of grace;
> Their look they cast back on the tempests,
>   On fears, on grim death and the grave,
> Rejoicing that now they're in safety,
>   Through Him that is mighty to save.
>
> And we, from the wilds of the desert,
>   Shall flee to the land of the blest;
> Life's tears shall be changed to rejoicing,
>   Its labours and toil into rest.
> There we shall find refuge eternal,
>   From sin, from affliction, from pain,
> And in the sweet love of the Saviour,
>   A joy without end shall attain.
>
> *David Charles, 1762–1834;*
> *translated by Lewis Edwards, 1809–87*

What reviewers have said

'This excellent book by one of our foremost preachers is a must for all committed to word ministry. The first reading of this book left me motivated to preach again, but with greater care, preparation and prayerful expectation. The clarity, precision and delightful forthrightness that we love in Stuart Olyott marks the book throughout. Nothing is complicated—it's all pure and simple!

'You may be tempted to think that this is a book for preachers alone, but hearers of sermons would be better equipped, after reading this book, to pray for the preacher week by week.'

Meirion Thomas (*The Evangelical Magazine*)

'I believe this is a necessary book, which is likely to do a power of good. All who preach need to strive for excellence, no matter how far off from it we seem to be. Those who are beginning to preach would do well to make this book a priority, it may save you from adopting methods you will need to unlearn and developing habits you have to shake off . . . Thank God for a helpful book like this, and pray for God's blessing upon those who read it.'

Grace Magazine

'Like the author this work is concise and precise . . . If it were in my power, I would get a copy of this book into the hands of every preacher not only for their encouragement, but also to enthuse them afresh in sermon preparation and delivery.'

Foundations

'For its size the best guide to preaching that this reviewer has ever seen. There should be a copy, if not many copies, in each church.'

Iain H. Murray (*The Banner of Truth*)

'Preaching—pure and simple is a book for all preachers in Africa, particularly for many of us who have never had a chance to go to Bible College. Since reading this book, I have realised how many times we have abused the pulpit by not preaching the Word . . . You may not understand how we always struggle when it comes to sermon preparation, but with such help as this we are able to meet the qualities needed in the preparation of the Word.'

Pastor Moses Kazefu, Zambia